The Complete
Rock & Pop
Guitar Player
Omnibus Edition

AMSCO PUBLICATIONS
A Part of the Music Sales Group
London / New York / Paris / Sydney / Copenhagen / Berlin / Madrid / Tokyo

PART 1

PART 2

PART 3

Exclusive Distributors:
Music Sales Corporation
257 Park Avenue South
New York, NY 10010, USA

Music Sales Limited
8/9 Frith Street
London W1D 3JB, England

Music Sales Pty Limited
120 Rothschild Avenue
Rosebery, Sydney, NSW 2018, Australia

Order Number: AM985809
This book © Copyright 2006 by Amsco Publications

Written and arranged by Rikky Rooksby.
Music processed by Paul Ewers.

Cover & book design by Fresh Lemon.
Cover photograph by George Taylor.
Artist photographs courtesy of
London Features International/ Redferns.

CD mastered by Jonas Persson.
Guitars by Arthur Dick.
Programming by John Moores and Chris Norton.

Printed in the United States of America by
Vicks Lithograph and Printing Corporation

Your Guarantee of Quality:
As publishers, we strive to produce every book to the
highest commercial standards. This book has been carefully
designed to minimize awkward page turns and to make
playing from it a real pleasure. Particular care has been
given to specifying acid-free, neutral-sized paper made from
pulps which have not been elemental chlorine-bleached.
This pulp is from farmed sustainable forests and was
produced with special regard for the environment.
Throughout, the printing and binding have been planned
to ensure a sturdy, attractive publication which should give
years of enjoyment. If your copy fails to meet our high
standards, please inform us and we will gladly replace it.

www.musicsales.com

The Complete Rock & Pop Guitar Player
Part 1

INTRODUCTION

Welcome to *The Complete Rock & Pop Guitar Player Part 1*. This is the first in a three-part course which can help you to play rock and pop guitar.

From the beginning this book teaches you to play classic songs faster than you thought possible. Just three chords and you can play along with tracks like "**No Woman, No Cry**," "**All Along the Watchtower**" and "**So Far Away**." You learn to play simply by following the easy strum patterns and chords written above the lyrics. You don't even have to read any music!

The songs are carefully graded, each one adding a new chord, a new strum pattern, or other technique. By the time you have finished **Part 1** you will have learned over 20 basic chords and many useful strum patterns. You will be ready to move on to more chords, strumming techniques, and some single-note playing in **Parts 2** and **3**.

THE GUITAR

To play the songs in this book you can use a nylon-string "classical" guitar, a steel-string acoustic, or an electric guitar. Of these the nylon-string guitar is not as effective for strumming. Its nylon strings won't produce quite as good a sound for rhythm guitar as steel strings. Nylon strings sound better with finger-style pieces.

Whether you have an acoustic or an electric guitar, the principles of playing are fundamentally the same, and so are most of the features on both instruments.

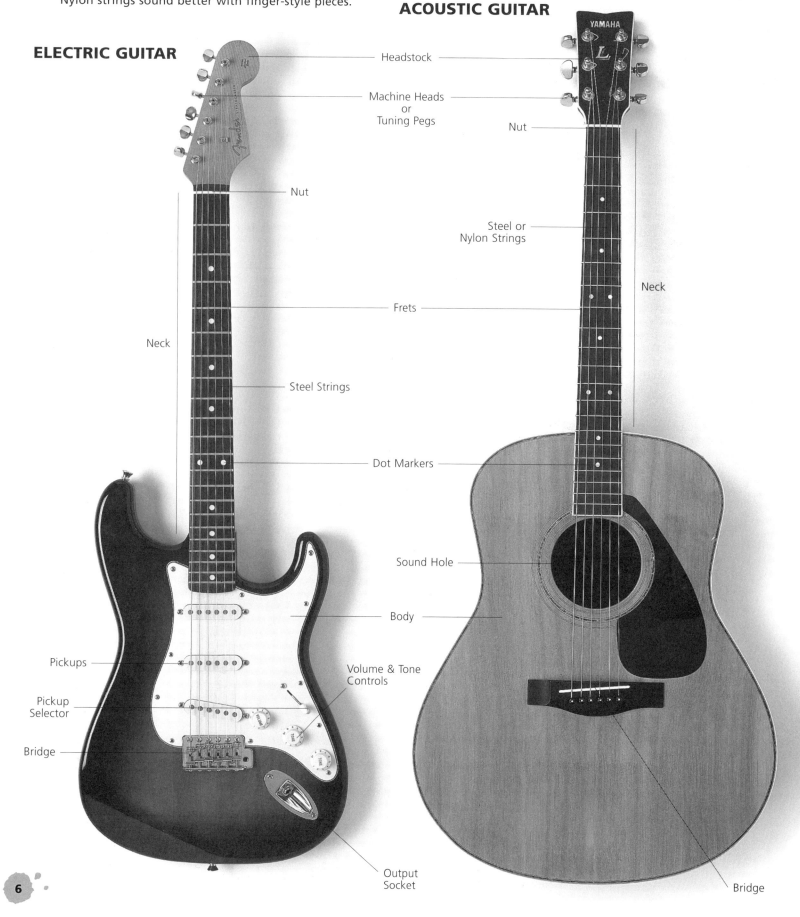

ACOUSTIC GUITAR

ELECTRIC GUITAR

Headstock

Machine Heads
or
Tuning Pegs

Nut

Nut

Neck

Steel or
Nylon Strings

Neck

Frets

Steel Strings

Dot Markers

Sound Hole

Body

Pickups

Volume & Tone
Controls

Pickup
Selector

Bridge

Output
Socket

Bridge

PLAYING THE GUITAR

The picture on the left shows a comfortable position for playing guitar.

THE RIGHT OR STRUMMING HAND

When strumming it is desirable to use a pick (or plectrum). You can use your thumb, or brush the strings with the nail-side of your fingers held together. However, a pick produces a more defined and clear sound.

THE LEFT OR FRETTING HAND

Use your fingertips to press down the strings in the positions described in this book. Your thumb should be behind your 1st and 2nd fingers, pressing on the middle of the back of the neck. It should retain its natural curve. In other words, don't bend it at the center thumb joint. Keep the thumb vertical. Never allow the flat of the palm of your fretting hand to touch the neck.

THE PICK

Picks come in many sizes, shapes and thicknesses, and are available from your local music store. The larger ones are easier to keep hold of, and for strumming you want one of the thinner types because these put up less resistance to the strings. The photo shows the correct way to hold your pick. Generally speaking, the thumb crosses behind the tip of the index finger at roughly a right angle to grip the pick.

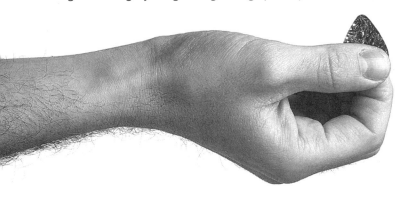

TUNING

Accurate tuning of the guitar is essential and is achieved by winding the machine heads up or down. It is always better to tune "up" to the correct pitch rather than down. Therefore, if you find that the pitch of your string is higher (sharper) than the correct pitch, you should "wind" down below the correct pitch and *then* tune up to it.

RELATIVE TUNING

Relative tuning simply means tuning the guitar to itself without the aid of a pitch pipe or other tuning device. Here's how to do it:

Estimate the pitch of the 6th string as near as possible to E, or at least a comfortable pitch (not too high, as you might break other strings when tuning up).

Then, while checking the various positions on the diagram below, place a finger from your fretting hand on:

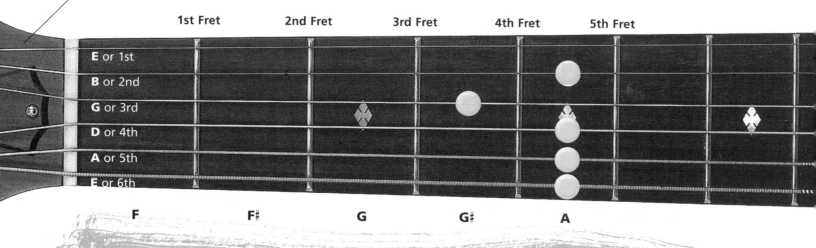

The 5th fret of the 6th string **E** and **tune the 5th string A** to the note produced, **A**

The 5th fret of the 5th string **A** and **tune the 4th string D** to the note **D**

The 5th fret of the 4th string **D** and **tune the 3rd string G** to the note **G**

The 4th fret of the 3rd string **G** and **tune the 2nd string B** to the note **B**

The 5th fret of the 2nd string **B** and **tune the 1st string E** to the note **E**

This is the most commonly used system for relative tuning. It's more accurate if you use a tuning fork, pitch pipe, piano, or **Track 1** on the CD to find the pitch of the 6th string **E**. However, all of the notes are given on our CD on **Track 1,** as a handy reference guide.

OTHER METHODS OF TUNING

Other ways to tune your guitar include using a pitch pipe, tuning fork, or an electronic tuner. These are all available from music stores.

CHORD BOXES

Chord boxes are diagrams of the guitar neck viewed head upward, face on, as illustrated in the diagram at right. The horizontal double line at the top represents the nut, and the other horizontal lines are the frets. The vertical lines are the strings, starting from the 6th **E** on the left, to the 1st **top E** on the right.

Any dots with numbers inside them simply indicate which finger goes where. Any strings marked with an **X** must not be played; strings marked with an **O** are played open.

The fingers of your fretting hand are numbered **1**, **2**, **3**, and **4** as on the photo below.

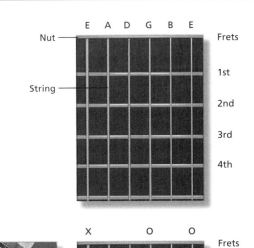

YOUR FIRST CHORD

The **C** chord.

Remember:

X Don't Play String

O Play Open String

C Chord

LEFT (OR FRETTING) HAND

Place all three fingers into position and press down firmly, just behind the metal fret wire. Keep your thumb near the middle of the back of the neck, behind your **2nd** finger.

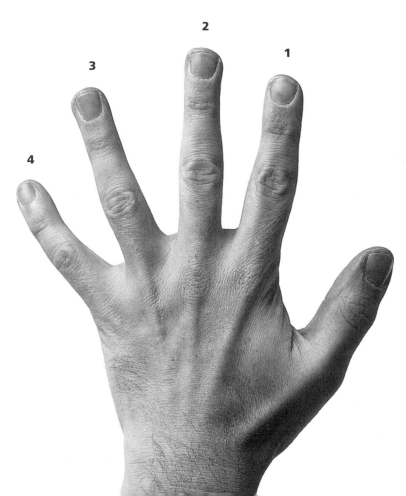

RIGHT-HAND THUMB OR PICK

Slowly play each string in the chord, starting with the 5th **A** string—notice that the bottom string has an **X** over it—and moving up to the 1st **E** string. If there is any buzzing, maybe you need to:

- **Position your fingers nearer the metal fret (toward you)**
- **Adjust the angle of your hand**
- **Check that the buzz is not elsewhere on the guitar by playing the open strings in the same way.**

Once you have a "buzz free" sound, play the chord a few times and then remove your fingers and repeat the exercise until your positioning is right instinctively.

USING A CAPO

Sometimes you will need to use a capo in order to play along with the songs in this book.

A capo is simply a small device that clamps across the guitar neck, to raise the pitch of all the strings together—useful for transposing songs or simplifying chords. They come in different forms, from cheap, basic ones, to more sturdy types. You can get one from any music store—it might be the most useful accessory you ever buy!

PAPERBACK WRITER
Words & Music by John Lennon & Paul McCartney

G Chord

To play this Beatles classic you need just two chords. Place your fingers in the correct positions and press down firmly. Remember to keep your thumb around the middle back of the neck and behind your 1st and 2nd fingers. Then follow the same procedure as you did for the C chord, this time starting with the 6th E string.

Check that all the strings are sounding cleanly by playing them one at a time. Then play the whole chord with a downstroke of your hand or pick.

Holding down the G chord, try strumming this rhythm using downstrokes. These are signified by a downward arrow. Try to keep your strums evenly spaced.

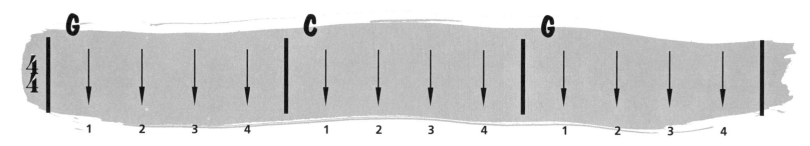

Well, if you want to sound technical you can say you have just played your first three bars of **4/4** time. Basically, **4/4** (four-four) time means four beats in a bar. These bars are separated by a barline, which marks the end of one bar and the beginning of another.

Now, still holding down your **G** chord, practice changing to **C** with your "four in a bar" rhythm, this time accentuating the first strum of every bar. It is best to play slowly and evenly at first, so that you have time to change chords without stopping.

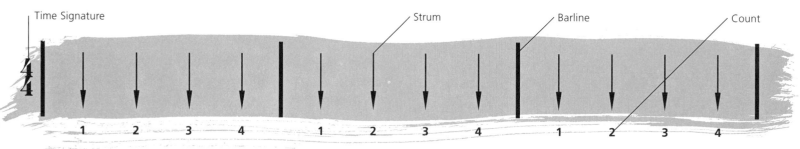

There is another way of fingering a **G** chord. By playing it with your **2nd**, **3rd,** and **4th** fingers you make it easier to change to **C** because your 1st finger is ready to go down on the 1st fret of the 2nd string, and the 2nd and 3rd fingers can keep their shape but just move across a string.

"Paperback Writer" has quite a fast tempo—but don't worry! You don't have to strum fast in this version. All you need to do is play downward on the chord on each first and third beat. The introduction consists of two bars of "clicks" followed by four bars of the famous guitar riff. Listen to the demonstration on **Track 2**, then play along. Don't rush ahead to the next song until you're confident with this one.

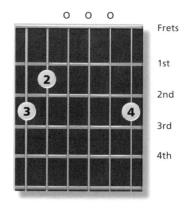

2 BAR CLICK INTRO

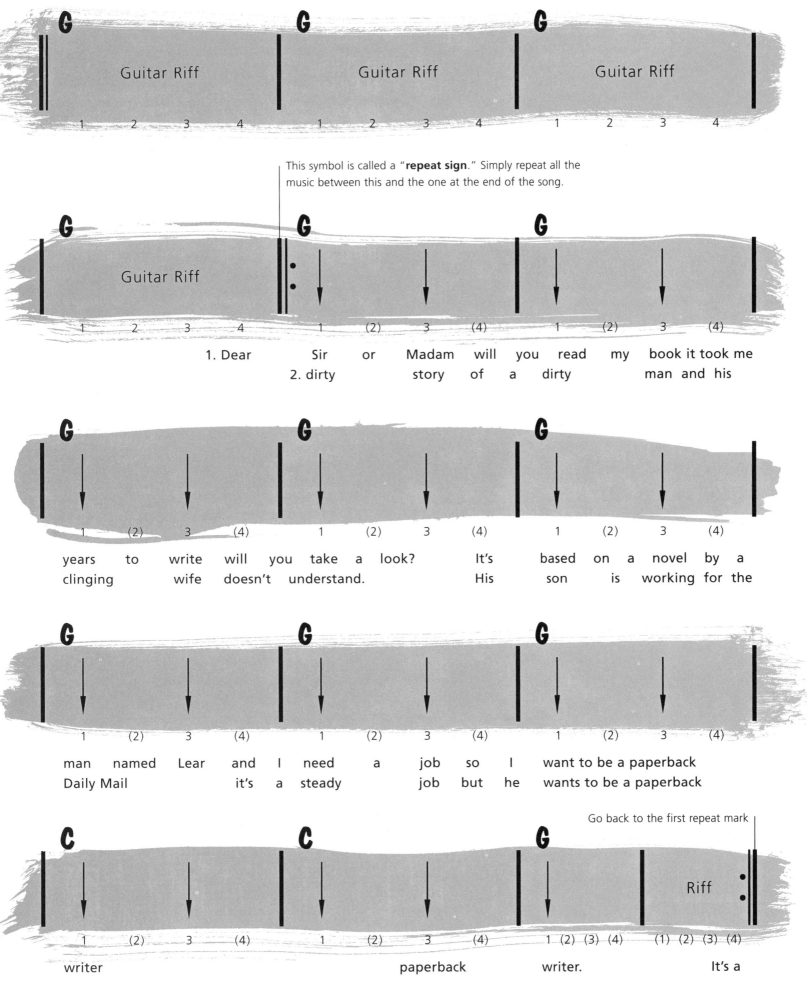

G   G   G

Guitar Riff   Guitar Riff   Guitar Riff

1 2 3 4   1 2 3 4   1 2 3 4

This symbol is called a "**repeat sign**." Simply repeat all the music between this and the one at the end of the song.

G   G   G

Guitar Riff

1 2 3 4   1 (2) 3 (4)   1 (2) 3 (4)

1. Dear   Sir   or   Madam will you read   my   book it took me
2. dirty   story of   a   dirty   man and his

G   G   G

1 (2) 3 (4)   1 (2) 3 (4)   1 (2) 3 (4)

years   to   write will you take a   look?   It's   based   on   a novel by a
clinging   wife doesn't understand.   His   son   is   working for the

G   G   G

1 (2) 3 (4)   1 (2) 3 (4)   1 (2) 3 (4)

man   named Lear   and   I   need   a   job   so   I   want to be a paperback
Daily Mail   it's   a steady   job   but   he   wants to be a paperback

Go back to the first repeat mark

C   C   G

1 (2) 3 (4)   1 (2) 3 (4)   1 (2) (3) (4)   (1) (2) (3) (4)

Riff

writer   paperback   writer.   It's a

BRIMFUL OF ASHA
Words & Music by Tjinder Singh

D Chord

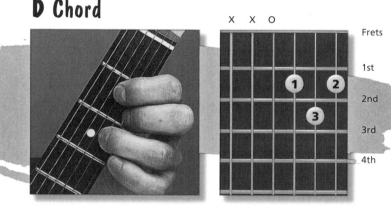

Indie-rock band Cornershop broke into the British music scene with this song in 1998. It went to No. 1 in the UK charts and No. 144 in the U.S.

Now it's time for you to learn your second tune, "Brimful Of Asha." We're going to learn one new chord and one new strumming pattern. The song has three basic parts—the verse, the chorus, and the bridge—and uses G, C, and D.

D major is played from the 4th string, which is **D**, the root note of the chord. When you strum it try to avoid hitting the 6th and 5th strings.

Instead of just strumming down on each beat, we will strum down *and* up on each beat. If you look at the first bar you'll see 1&2& etc. written under the words. Tap your foot four times in each bar and on the first tap count "1&," on the second tap "2&" and so on. The number is the downstroke and the "&" is the upstroke. Upstrokes may seem a little strange at first but you will soon get accustomed to them. You will notice the benefit of strumming with a soft pick when you do upstrokes.

The original version is in **A major**. Since **A major** is one step (two frets) higher than **G major**, all you have to do is put a capo on the second fret of the guitar and use the **G**, **C** and **D** shapes. After you learn the chords for **A** and **E** you can come back and try playing "Brimful" without the capo to compare the sound. (Without a capo, for a **G** play **A**, for **C** play **D** and for **D** play **E**.)

CAPO 2ND FRET
8 BAR INTRO

Look out for the repeat signs!

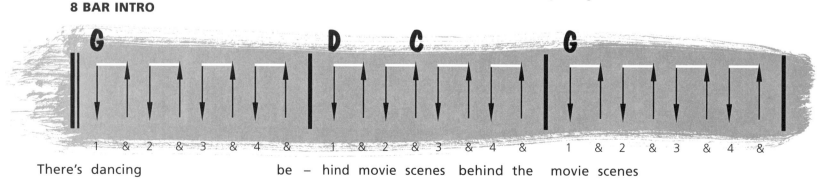

G				D	C		G		
1	&	2	&	3	&	4	&		

There's dancing   be – hind movie scenes behind the   movie scenes

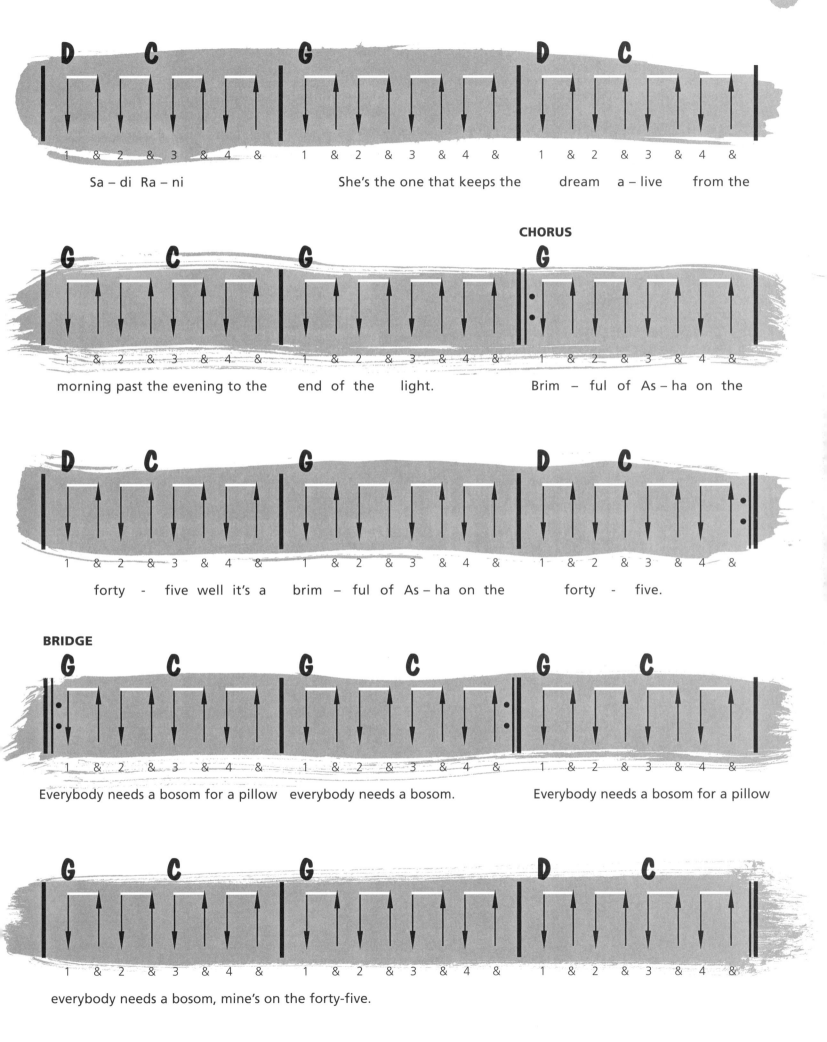

TWO TICKETS TO PARADISE
Words & Music by Eddie Money

Two Tickets To Paradise" reached No. 22 in the US charts in 1978 and featured on Eddie's multi-platinum self-titled album. It requires one new chord, A major, played from the 5th string, which is A, the root of the chord.

Start by placing your 1st finger on the 2nd fret of the 4th string and then locate the other finger positions. If you find it a problem squeezing all three fingers into the space, you can always try using the 2nd, 3rd, and 4th (so that the 4th is on the 2nd string).

The strum pattern is the same for "**Brimful Of Asha**," down and up on each beat. Each of these strums represents the rhythm value of an 8th note. So we can call this a strum in straight 8ths.

A Chord

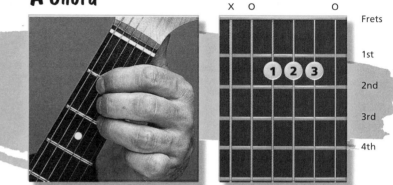

Notice that when you change from **A** to **D** your 3rd finger does not need to lift off the 2nd string; it only needs to move back or forward one fret. This is called a "guide finger." Spotting a guide finger—a finger that moves along a string and therefore does not have to lift off—will help you change chords faster.

VERSE

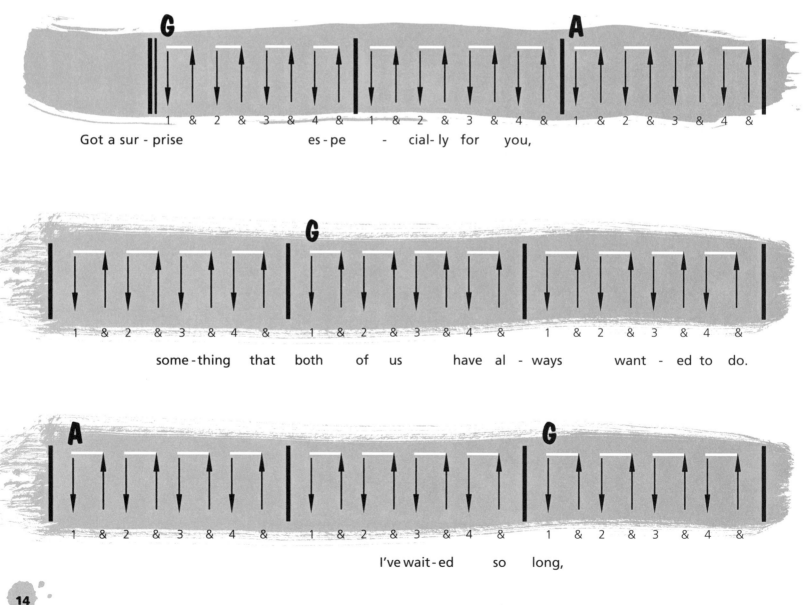

Got a sur-prise   es-pe - cial-ly for you,

some-thing   that   both   of   us   have al - ways   want - ed to do.

I've wait-ed   so   long,

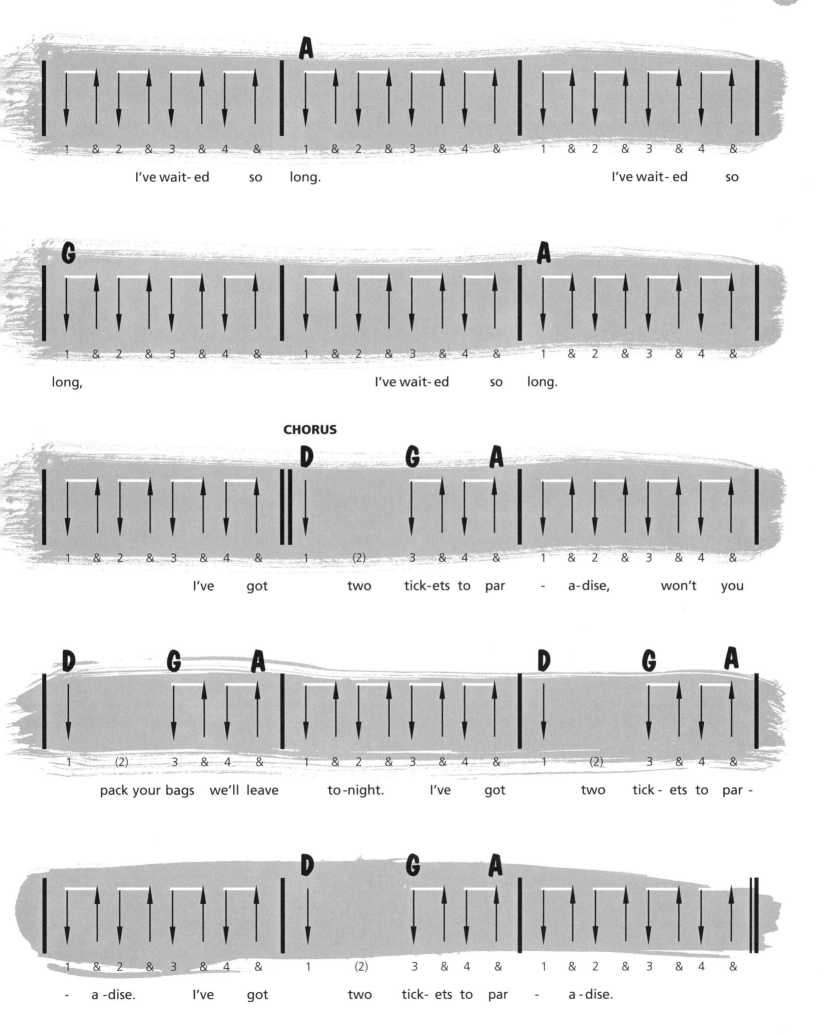

ROCK AROUND THE CLOCK
Words & Music by Max C. Freedman & Jimmy De Knight

Bill Haley and His Comets' "Rock Around The Clock" helped start a revolution in popular music in 1955. Featured in the film *Blackboard Jungle*, it sold millions worldwide and turned people on to rock'n'roll.

E Chord

This song spent eight weeks at No. 1 and was the most successful Rock'n'Roll record of all time!

Many rock'n'roll songs use a verse structure called a "twelve-bar," taken from the blues but played at a quicker tempo. If you count the bars from the start of the verse you will find "**Rock Around The Clock**" has twelve bars and just three chords. Yes, it's **A**, **D** and a new chord, **E**.

E major is a significant chord on the guitar. Easy to play, it allows you to hit all six strings and to have the open 6th string—the guitar's lowest note—sounding. No other major chord on the guitar sounds quite like **E**!

For the intro, only strike the chords on the beats marked. There are gaps where there is only the voice. Since "**Rock Around The Clock**" is fast, we are going to use a single (quarter note) strum to each beat, with occasional upstrokes on the third offbeats.

When you get confident with the chord changes you can experiment with strumming 8ths, down and up on each beat. However, because the song uses a "swing" rhythm, it is as if the beat is divided into three rather than two. Instead of straight 8ths, where the two strums are rhythmically equal, in a "swing rhythm" song the first strum is twice as long as the second. Tap your foot in a steady 4/4 time and say "1 2 3" on each beat instead of "1 &." Your first strum will be down on "1" and up on "3." Practice this slowly at first.

2 BAR CLICK INTRO

♩♩ = ♩♪ This means "swing rhythm"

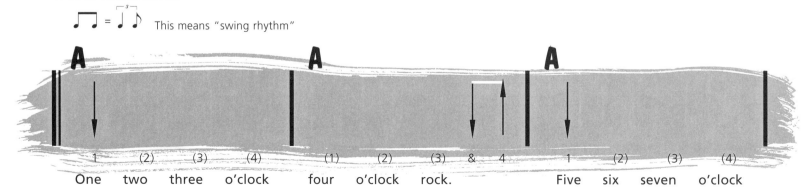

A				A					A			
1	(2)	(3)	(4)	(1)	(2)	(3)	&	4	1	(2)	(3)	(4)
One	two	three	o'clock	four		o'clock		rock.	Five	six	seven	o'clock

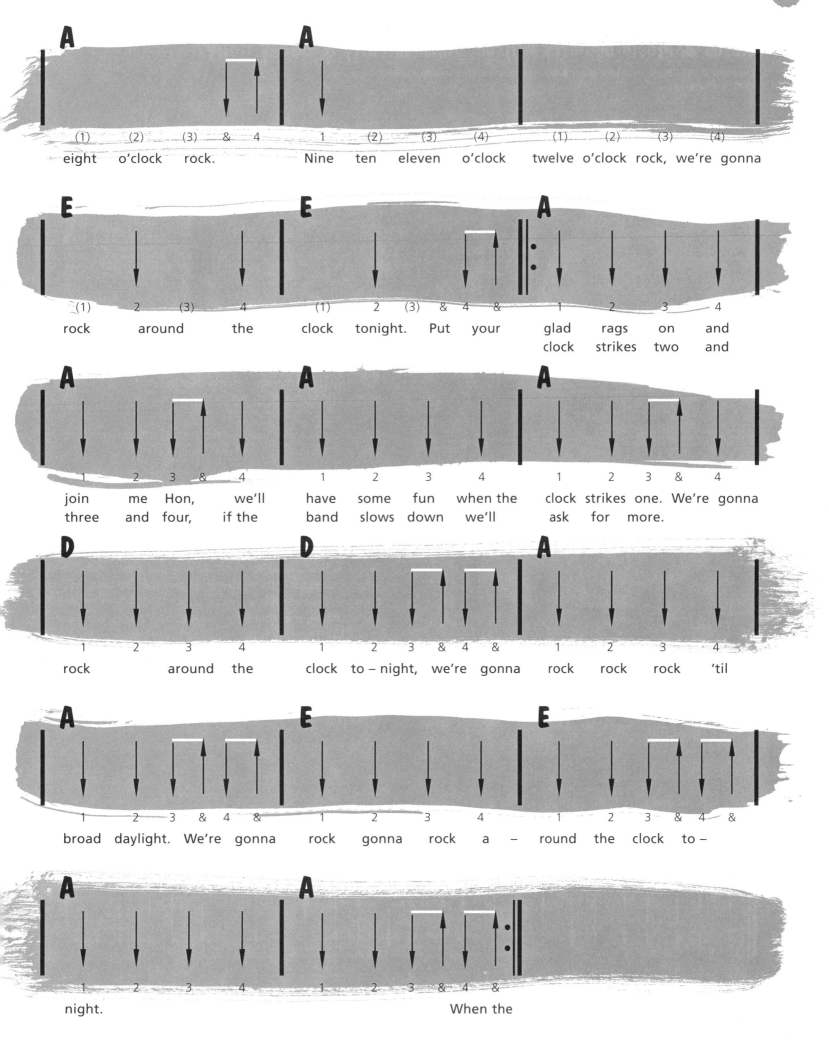

THAT'LL BE THE DAY
Words & Music by Jerry Allison, Norman Petty & Buddy Holly

B7 Chord

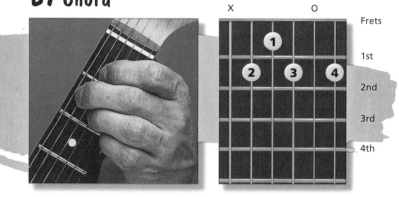

This song was the title song to the 1970's movie That'll Be The Day.

One new chord is needed for this rock'n'roll standard from Buddy Holly and the Crickets, a No.1 in 1957.

B7 is actually easier to play than a straight **B major** chord, even though it is slightly more complex.

Like "**Rock Around The Clock**," "**That'll Be The Day**" has a swing feel, so when you strum the 8ths they are not equal pairs. Each downstroke on the beat lasts roughly twice as long as the upstroke on the offbeat.

Take a look at bar 7. You'll notice only one arrow in the bar. What this means is that you should play the first beat only, then mute the strings while you count "2, 3, 4." In the next bar, you'll see that there is no down arrow on the first beat of the bar. This means that you don't play beat 1, but instead start strumming on the "&" with an upstroke.

Watch out also for the last bar—here you strum three times on each beat. Three notes played in the time of one are called triplets.

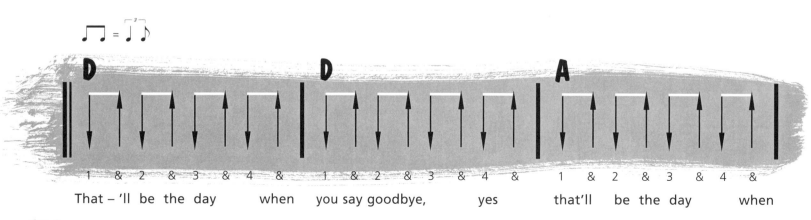

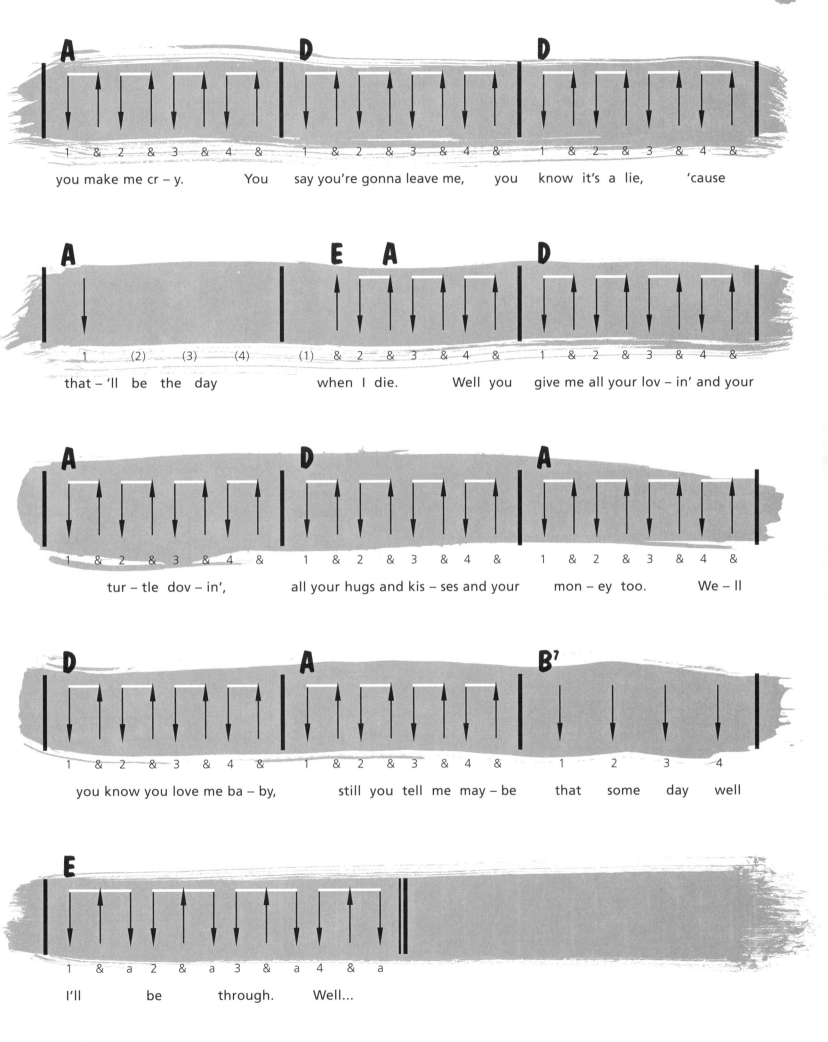

I WANNA BE ADORED

Words & Music by Ian George Brown & John Squire

Em Chord

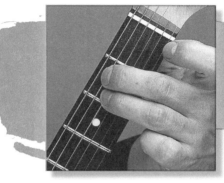
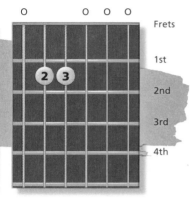

Frets
1st
2nd
3rd
4th

This atmospheric track by The Stone Roses is one of the stand-out songs of their 1989 debut album. There is one new chord for this song, E minor.

Like **E major**, **E minor** is effective because it uses all six strings and the lowest note on the guitar. This gives **E minor** its characteristic deep, resonant tone. If you compare it with **E** (by putting your first finger on the **1st fret** of the **3rd string**), you can hear the difference in tone. In contrast with major chords, minor chords sound sad.

"**I Wanna Be Adored**" gives us the opportunity to experiment with a new strumming pattern.

The original track begins with a long instrumental passage featuring a strong "chugging" 8th-note rhythm. You could play the whole song in this way, with straight 8th notes (as in the first two bars). However, to make things a little more interesting, let's try the pattern in bars three and four. This pattern uses ties—see page 87. Break it down by counting really slowly: 1 2 3 & 4 & (1) & 2 & (3) & 4 &. Count, but don't play, the numbers in brackets—they are there to help you keep your place.

This is the first really challenging rhythm you've had, so take your time and get it right! The song starts with a four-bar fade in.

This track was released in 1991 and features John Squire at his best... big atmospheric catchy riffs.

4 BAR FADE IN

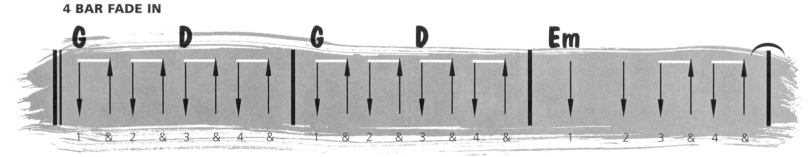

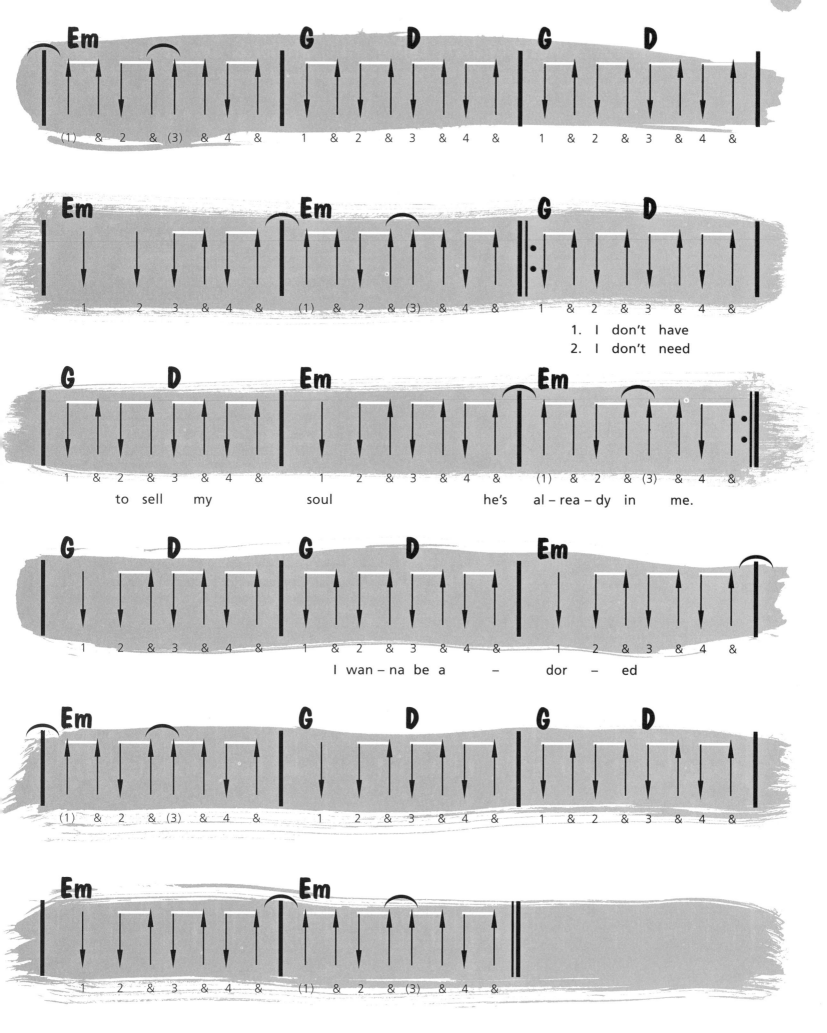

STAND BY ME
Words & Music by Jerry Leiber, Mike Stoller & Ben E. King

Let's use the same four chords for another song. "Stand By Me" has been released by a number of artists and has been featured in many film and ad campaigns. Ben E. King had a hit with it in 1961 and in 1987 it was featured in a Levi's TV ad. In between, in 1975 John Lennon released a well-known version from his album *Rock'n'Roll*.

Up to now we have had a maximum of two strums per beat and we have been counting 1 & 2 & 3 & 4 & for each bar. If you look at the first beat of each bar you will see there is an extra strum between the "&" sign and the "2." Count this extra strum as an "a."

So, the rhythm of each bar is counted like this: 1 &-a-2 & 3 & 4 &. Remember, you must arrive at the "2" on the second foot tap so you have to squeeze the "a" strum in between the "&" and the "2."The extra strum is pretty fast, so practice it slowly first.

Our recording features the full introduction, which is eight bars of music, plus two bars of click—10 bars in total. Listen to the intro and see if you can tell when to come in—if not, our guitar demo will show you. Learning to count "empty bars" (i.e., bars you aren't playing in) is a valuable skill.

John Lennon's classic 1975 version was the last of several collaborations with the legendary producer and eccentric inventor of the "Wall Of Sound," Phil Spector.

CAPO 2ND FRET
2 BAR CLICK + 8 BAR INTRO

G | G | Em

1 & a 2 & 3 & 4 & 1 & a 2 & 3 & 4 & 1 & a 2 & 3 & 4 &

When the night   has   come,   and the land   is

Em | C | D

1 & a 2 & 3 & 4 & 1 & a 2 & 3 & 4 & 1 & a 2 & 3 & 4 &

dark,   and the moon   is   the on – ly   light we'll

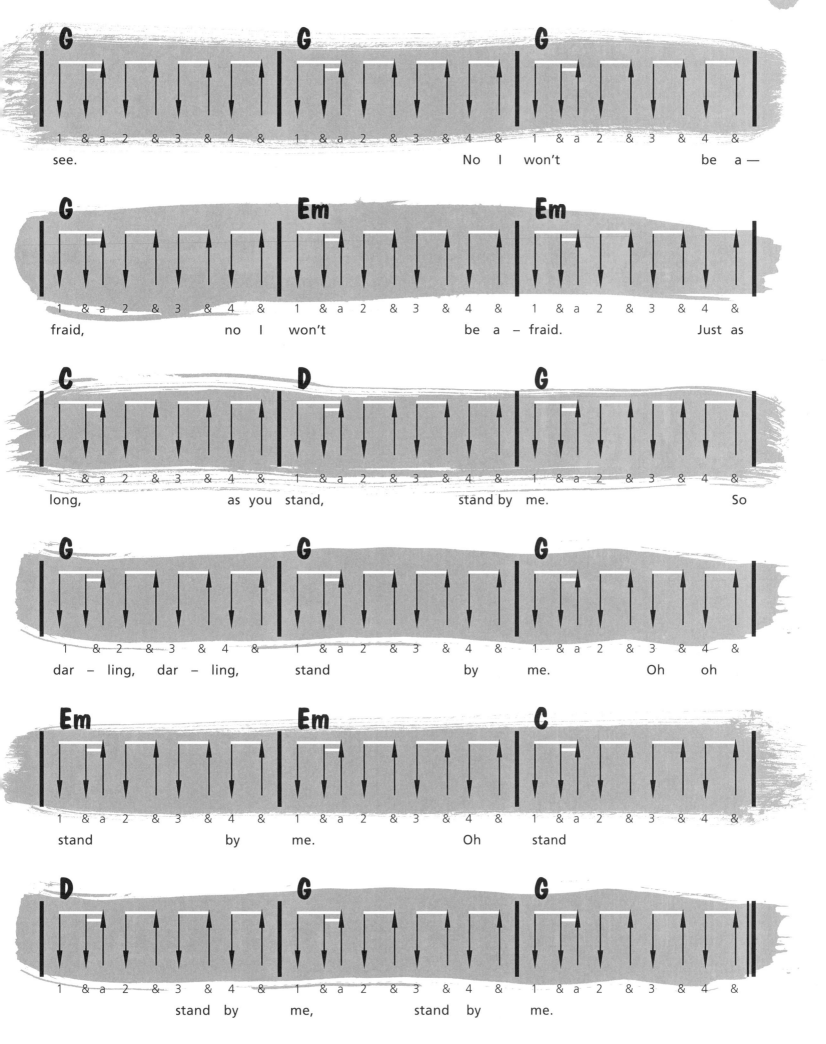

CATHY'S CLOWN
Words & Music by Don Everly

If you have a friend who can sing harmony now is the time to call them up! The next song is a classic of two-voice singing— The Everly Brothers' "Cathy's Clown," which went to No.1 on both sides of the Atlantic in 1960.

Surprisingly, given the very different themes of the songs, it uses the same chords—**G**, **C**, **D** and **Em**—as "**I Wanna Be Adored**" and "**Stand By Me**."

The strumming is quite easy. During the chorus, use downstrokes on the beat, keeping the notes short. In the verse, when the rhythm changes, strum down and up on each beat. Watch out for the rests at bar 12 and 16!

The Everly Brothers - The Harmony Brothers?

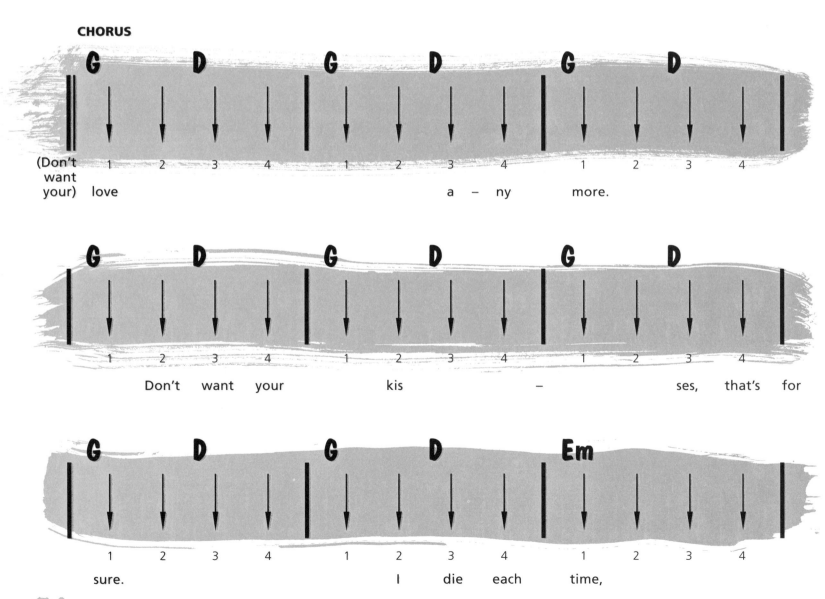

CHORUS

| G | D | G | D | G | D |

(Don't want your) love   a – ny more.

| G | D | G | D | G | D |

Don't want your kis – ses, that's for

| G | D | G | D | Em |

sure.   I die each time,

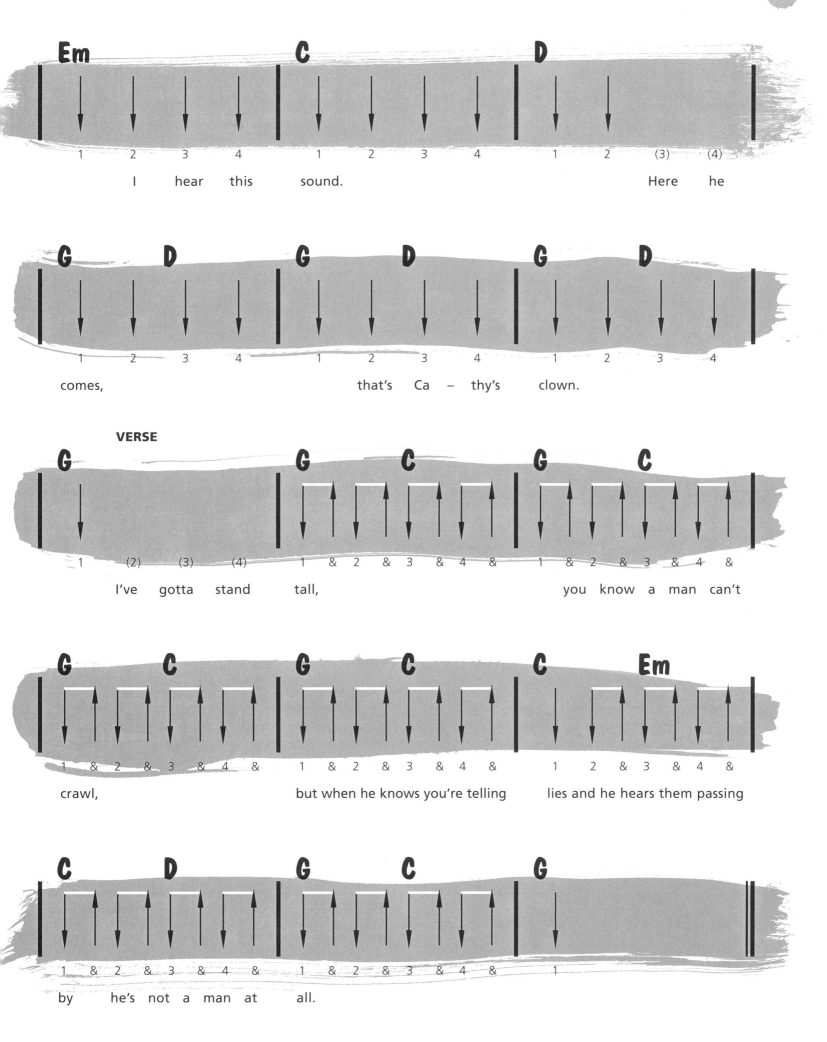

Jarvis Cocker—getting back to nature. Word is, his "forest" gigs are selling out like wildfire...

COMMON PEOPLE

Words & Music by Nick Banks, Jarvis Cocker, Candida Doyle, Stephen Mackey & Russell Senior

How easy or hard you find barre chords depends on several things. First, if the strings on your guitar are too high off the fretboard they will be harder to hold down. Second, you need to keep the first finger quite straight. You may find it easier if you drop the thumb of your fretting hand a little lower behind the neck. A **barre** is not entirely brute strength, there's also a positioning element, so re-position your first finger if you find the strings are lining up with the grooves behind the finger-joints. You should also try to apply pressure with the first finger slightly rolled toward the nut, so that the bonier edge of the finger makes a bit more contact.

Don't worry if the full **F** seems hard at first. Try the second chord box instead, an abbreviated version with a half barre across the top two strings.

One of the more unusual British acts to hit the British charts in the 1990s was Pulp. To play their 1995 single "Common People" we need the chords **C** and **G**, which you already know, plus one more: **F major.**

F barre Chord

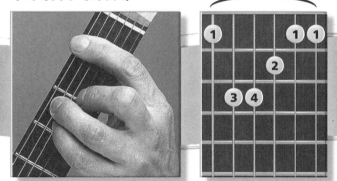

The chords you have learned so far—**C G D A E B7** and **Em**—all have open strings. With **F** major all the strings you strum are fretted with your fingers. One result of this is that you can move the shape up and down the neck to make different major chords. For instance, if you moved your hand to the 2nd fret with this shape you would have the chord of **F♯/G♭** major.

F (half barre) Chord

Most of the strumming in "**Common People**" is in 8ths, but to add more interest it can sometimes be a good idea to leave gaps. There are many bars in "**Common People**" where you strum down on the 1st beat but not up on the offbeat.

4 BAR INTRO

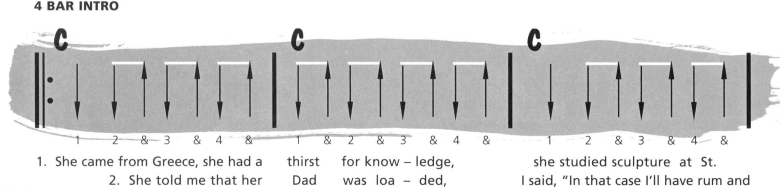

1. She came from Greece, she had a thirst for know – ledge, she studied sculpture at St.
2. She told me that her Dad was loa – ded, I said, "In that case I'll have rum and

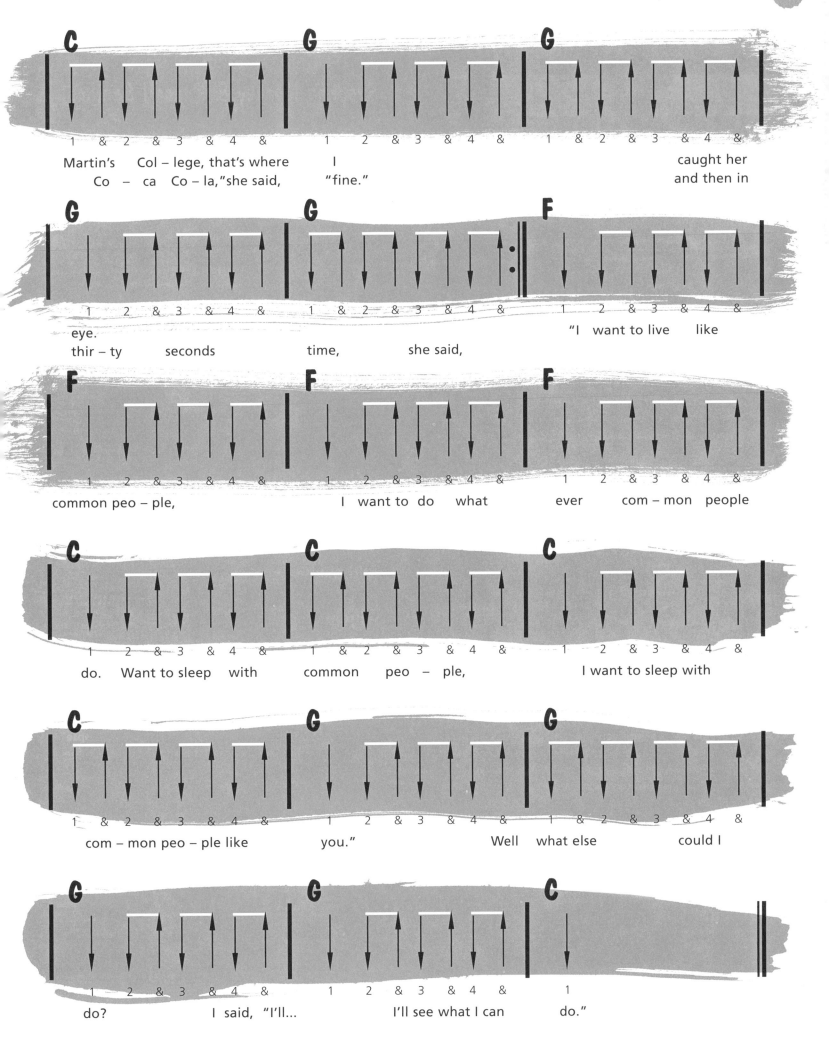

ALL ALONG THE WATCHTOWER
Words & Music by Bob Dylan

Although originally recorded by Bob Dylan on *John Wesley Harding* (1968) and covered by U2 on *Rattle and Hum* (1988), "All Along The Watchtower" is most closely associated with legendary 60s guitarist Jimi Hendrix.

A minor Chord

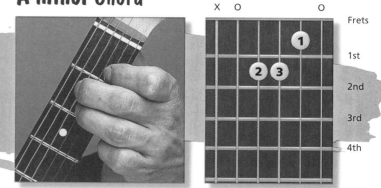

Although Jimi's recording on *Electric Ladyland* is a staggering display of guitar skills, the basics of the song are very simple. **"All Along The Watchtower"** gives you another opportunity to try **F**, and you need one new chord: **A minor**.

Like **E minor**, **A minor** has a sad, melancholy sound. It doesn't seem as deep in tone because the 6th string is not played; the root is the open **A** string. One way of remembering the shape is to think of an **E** chord that has been moved down one string. Can you see the resemblance? If you play a song with a change from **Am** to **E** you'll see that it's an easy change because the fingers don't change their shape, only move across the strings.

The intro uses the same strum pattern as in **"I Wanna Be Adored,"** where there is no strum on the third beat. Notice also that in all the even numbered bars the change from **F** to **G** occurs on the 3rd offbeat.

If you find the **F** chord hard, try using the half-barre shape instead (see page 26).

To play along with the original, put a capo at the 3rd fret.

They say other people have more success with Dylan's songs than he did... well it's certainly true in this case!

CAPO 3RD FRET

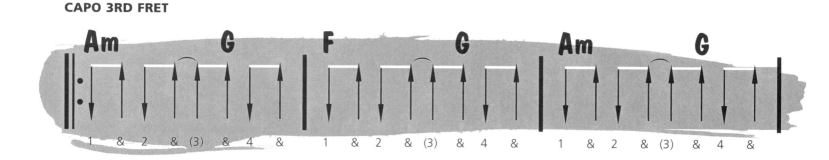

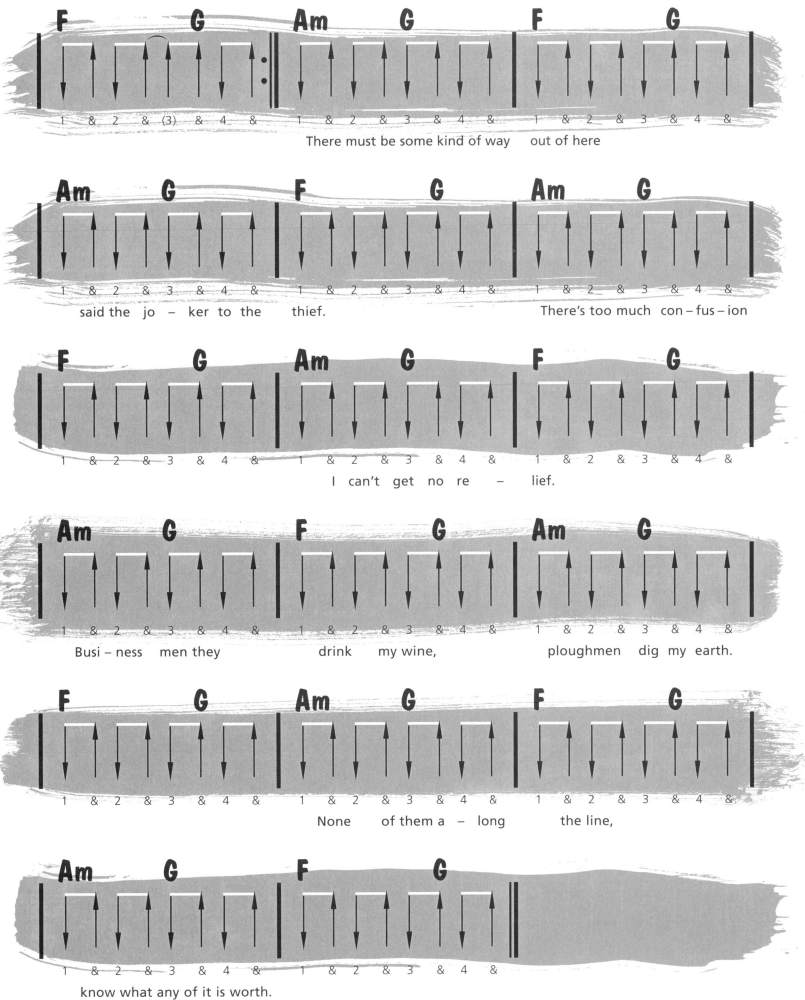

There must be some kind of way   out of here

said the jo – ker to the   thief.   There's too much con – fus – ion

I can't get no re – lief.

Busi – ness   men they   drink   my wine,   ploughmen dig my earth.

None   of them a – long   the line,

know what any of it is worth.

NO WOMAN, NO CRY
Words & Music by Vincent Ford

Bob Marley was reggae's first superstar. He and his band The Wailers achieved this status with a series of hit records that included a live album from a concert at the Lyceum in London in 1975. The atmosphere of that gig is captured on "No Woman, No Cry."

This song uses four chords—**C**, **Am**, **F**, and **G**—which you have played before. However, the **G** chord is found in a slightly different form. If you found the **F barre** chord hard then **G/B** will be a relief because you only need to use one finger!

G/B Chord

x   o   o   o   x

Frets
1st
2nd
3rd
4th

"Me really love 'No Woman, No Cry' because it mean so much to me. Me get so much feeling from it." Bob Marley

This type of chord is known as an "inversion." All this means is that the root note (the note after which a chord is named) is not the lowest. One of the other two notes that make a simple major or minor chord is at the bottom. In **G/B, B** is the lowest note.

Inversions often occur in chord sequences when the songwriter wants an ascending or descending bass line. **G/B** is popular on the guitar because it is easy to play, and almost always found, as here, between **C** and **Am**.

The strumming is mostly slow 8ths, but look at bar 2. Notice there is no down strum on the 3rd beat. Instead, the **F** is played on the offbeat of the previous 2nd beat. This type of change, coming half a beat before you expect it, is known as an "anticipation." Anticipated changes are very important in many forms of popular music. They help to create more of a "groove." Listen for the way the **F** chord "hangs" across the pause in the strumming. If you find the **F** chord hard, use the half-barre version.

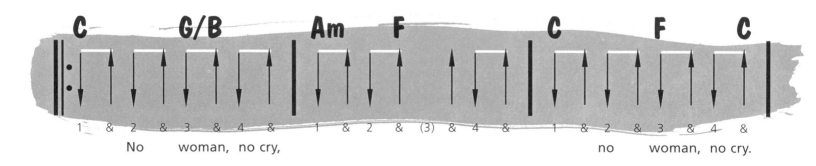

No   woman, no cry,   no   woman, no cry.

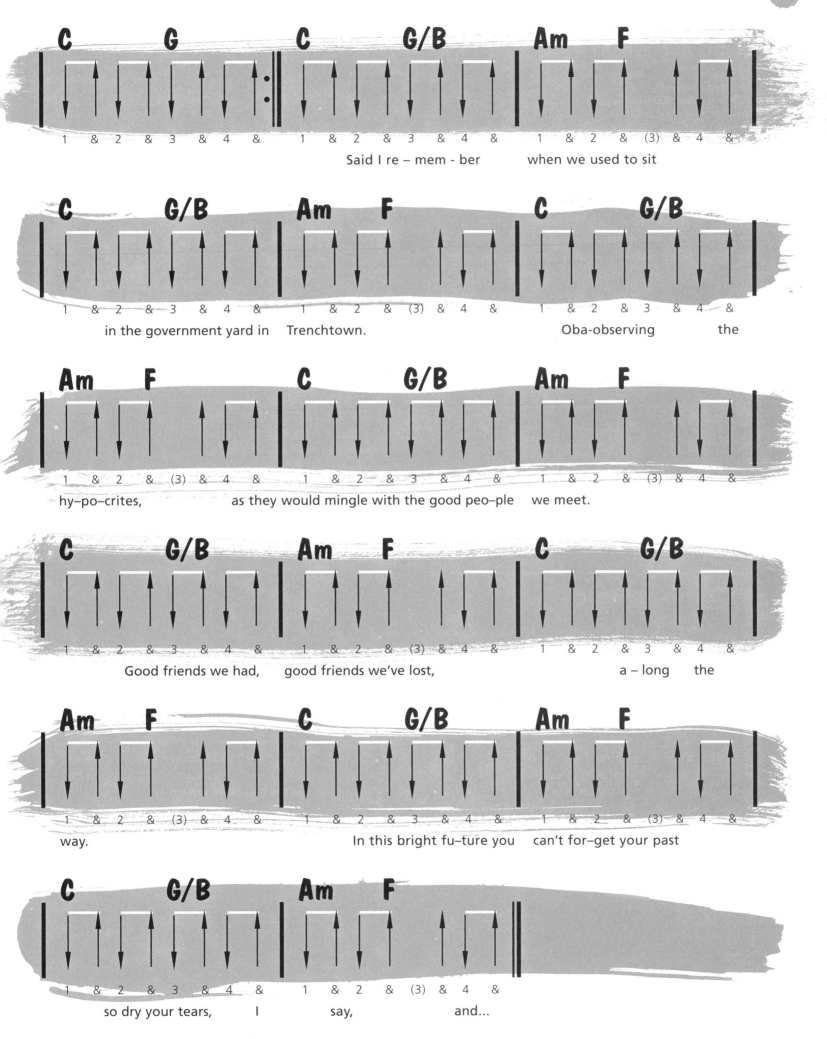

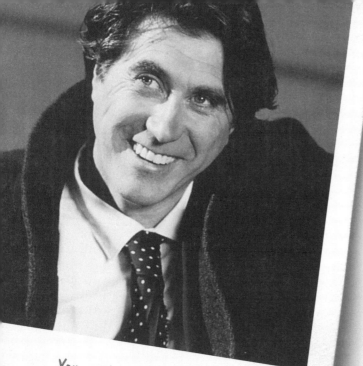

DANCE AWAY
Words & Music by Bryan Ferry

B minor Chord

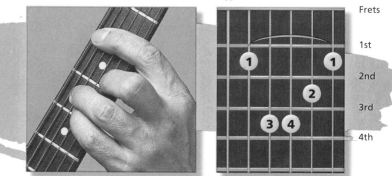

There are no open strings in **Bm**, and it is one of the most important moveable minor shapes. Move it up one fret and it becomes **C minor**, down a fret it becomes **B♭ minor**.

Remember to keep your thumb down low behind the neck for a barre shape such as this. Play each string individually to make sure that all are sounding.

"Dance Away" uses one strum pattern. Strum down on the 1st beat, wait for the 2nd and then continue with 8ths. To play along with the original, put a capo at the 3rd fret.

You can hear the original version of this song on Roxy Music's 1979 album Manifesto.

To play this elegant Roxy Music hit from 1979 you need a new minor chord: B minor. This shape is actually derived from Am.

CAPO 3RD FRET

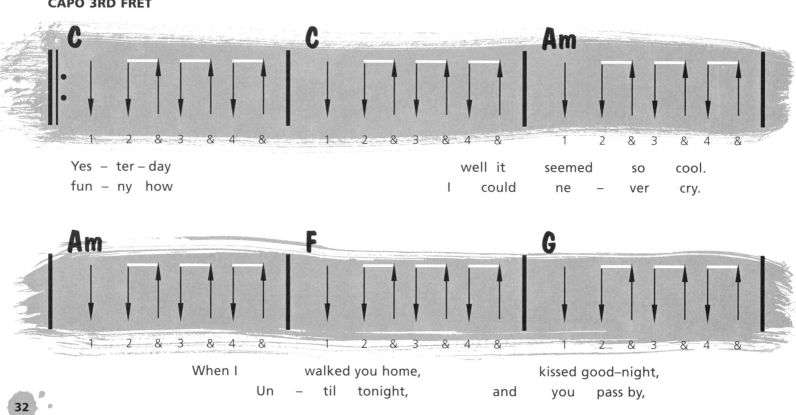

Yes – ter – day well it seemed so cool.
fun – ny how I could ne – ver cry.

When I walked you home, kissed good–night,
Un – til tonight, and you pass by,

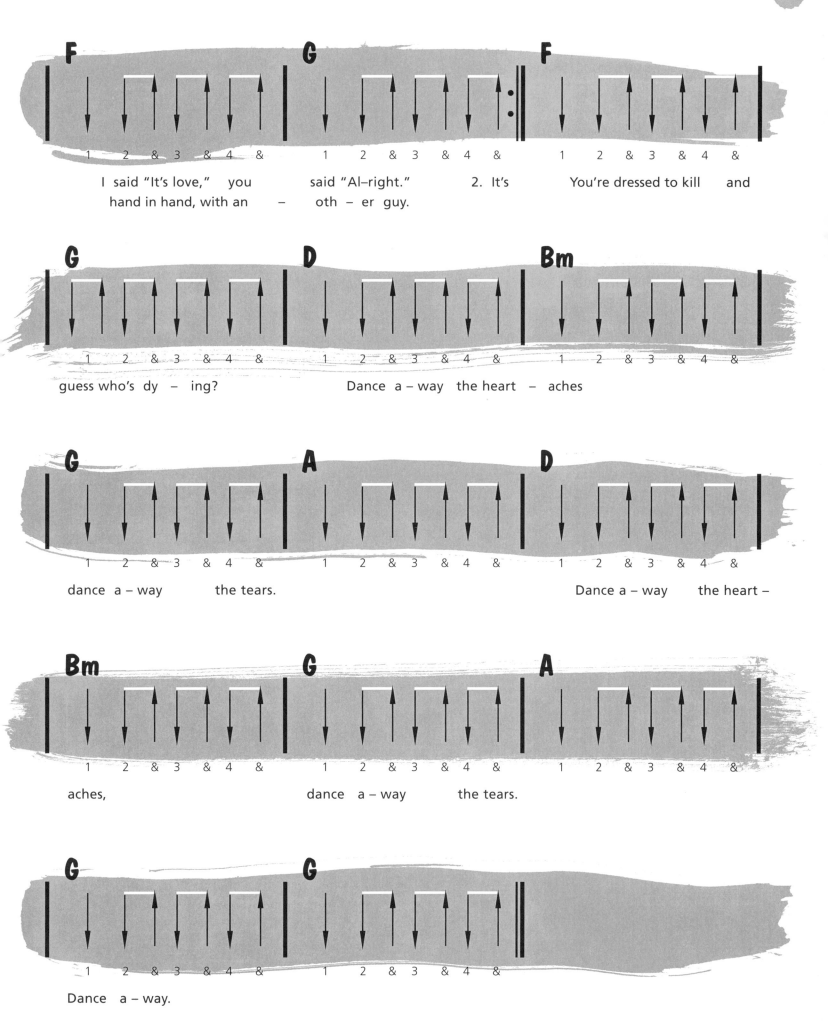

THAT'S ENTERTAINMENT
Words & Music by Paul Weller

Am7 Chord

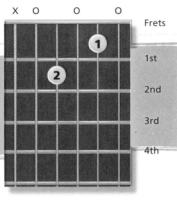

Em7 Chord

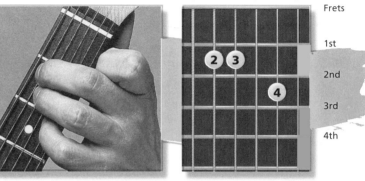

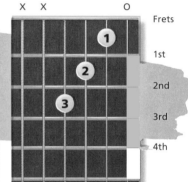

In 1980, Paul Weller wrote this hit song, signifying a shift away from The Jam's trademark aggressive power chords.

Fmaj7 Chord

"**That's Entertainment**" manages to combine a haunting lyric with a driving acoustic rhythm and uses only five chords. You already know **G** and **Em**. The three new chords are variations on **Am, Em,** and **F** and they're all very easy.

Em7 is easy—you can play **Em** and then add your fourth finger. Notice how adding the 7th "softens" the sound of the minor chord—now it doesn't sound as sad.

Am7 is simply **Am** with the third finger lifted off. Let the open strings ring out, but beware not to let the bottom E string sound.

Fmaj7 is the same as the **F** half barre, but without the barre. Let the 1st string ring open and be careful not to strum the bottom strings.

You'll see that on the last beat of some of the bars there's that quick 16th up-and-down figure that you first tried out with "**Stand By Me**." Listen for the effect of the even-numbered bars where **Em7** turns into **Em** as you lift your little finger off the 2nd string.

Like the original recording, the CD track for "**That's Entertainment**" features a capo at the 3rd fret.

The intro is 8 bars long—again, practice counting to find out where you should start playing.

Paul Weller — a Modern Classic.

2 BAR CLICK + 8 BAR INTRO
CAPO 3RD FRET

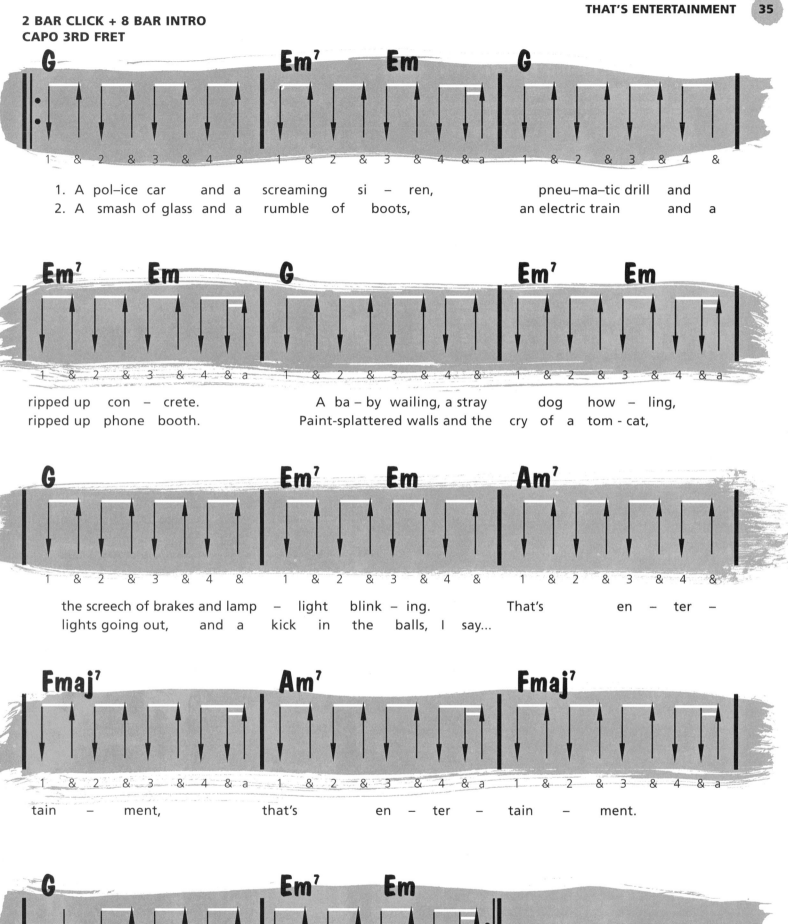

1. A pol–ice car and a screaming si – ren, pneu–ma–tic drill and
2. A smash of glass and a rumble of boots, an electric train and a

ripped up con – crete. A ba – by wailing, a stray dog how – ling,
ripped up phone booth. Paint-splattered walls and the cry of a tom - cat,

the screech of brakes and lamp – light blink – ing. That's en – ter –
lights going out, and a kick in the balls, I say...

tain – ment, that's en – ter – tain – ment.

THE TIDE IS HIGH

By John Holt, Tyrone Evans & Howard Barrett

Blondie's version of "The Tide Is High" reached No. 1 in 1980. Here, it introduces the chord of B major. The B major chord like, the Bm chord, is derived from the shape for A.

If you find this difficult you can simplify it by taking the barre off. Then the 1st finger just holds down the 2nd fret of the top string. If you play B this way you must be careful not to strum either the 5th or 6th strings. Along with the full **F**, **B** is the most important moveable major barre shape.

This song has a slight reggae feel, which is achieved by strumming on the offbeats only. Count silently on each beat (the numbers in brackets), and play a short upstroke on each "&" for a steady (1) & (2) & (3) & (4) & groove. The **F♯** in the second measure is the same as the **F** barre chord you learned earlier, just moved up to the 2nd fret. Stay on the 2nd fret for the change back to the **B** chord.

B major Chord

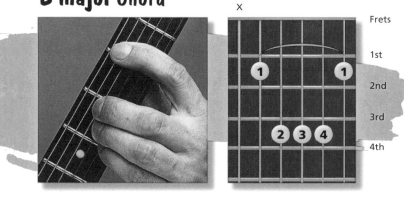

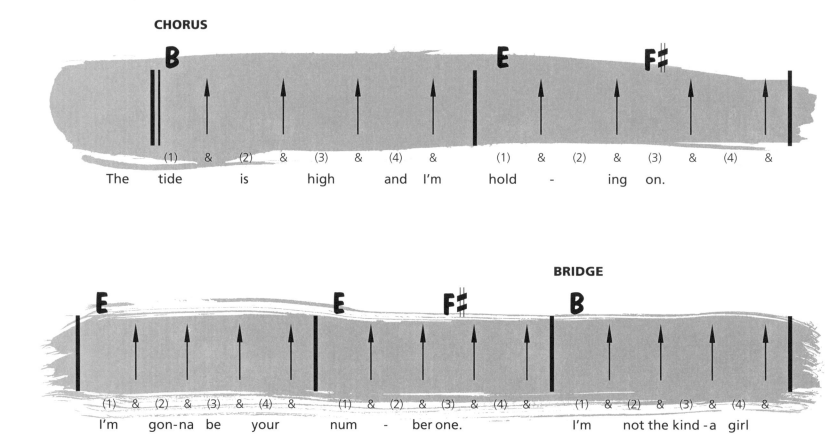

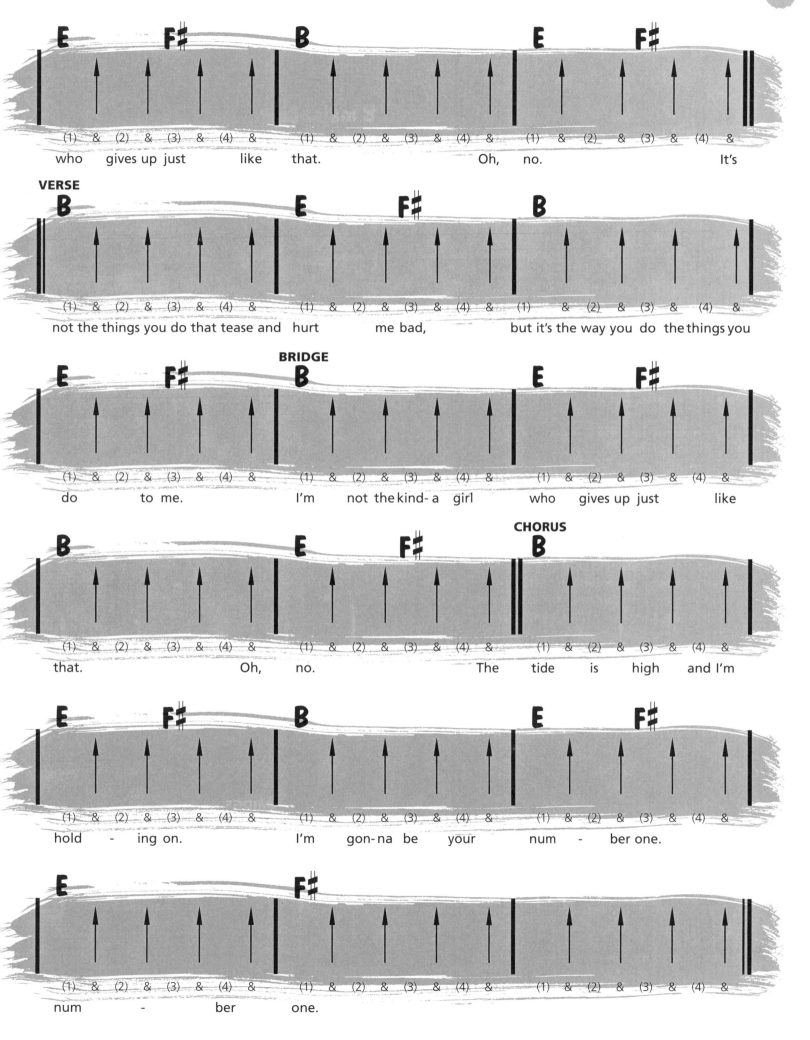

SO FAR AWAY
Words & Music by Mark Knopfler

C#m Chord

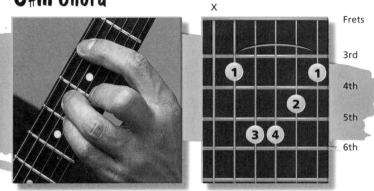

This track from Dire Straits' best-selling album *Brothers In Arms* features an easy, relaxed strum, and one new chord: C#m.

The **C# minor** chord is the **B minor** chord moved up two frets. If you find this difficult you can simplify it by taking the barre off. Then the 1st finger just holds down the 4th fret of the top string. If you play **C#m** this way you must be careful not to strum either the 5th or 6th strings.

To emulate the chugging 8th-note rhythm of the original, try **damping** the chords. You do this by resting the side of your strumming hand on the strings very close to the tailpiece (where the strings are fixed to the body). Don't make too much contact or the strings won't make enough sound. If you get it right it just takes the ring out of them. Then you can concentrate on hitting the lower notes of each chord.

When you change from **C#m** to **B** to **E** in the chorus, watch your 3rd finger on the fretting hand. It's a guide finger. Notice that it does not go to a *different* string; it goes down the 4th string.

Mark Knopfler's trademark bottleneck licks have always been instantly recognizable — and this track is no exception.

VERSE

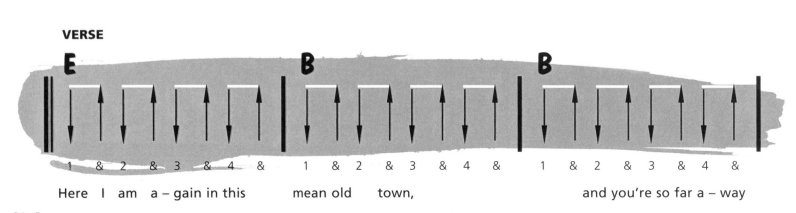

Here I am a – gain in this   mean old   town,   and you're so far a – way

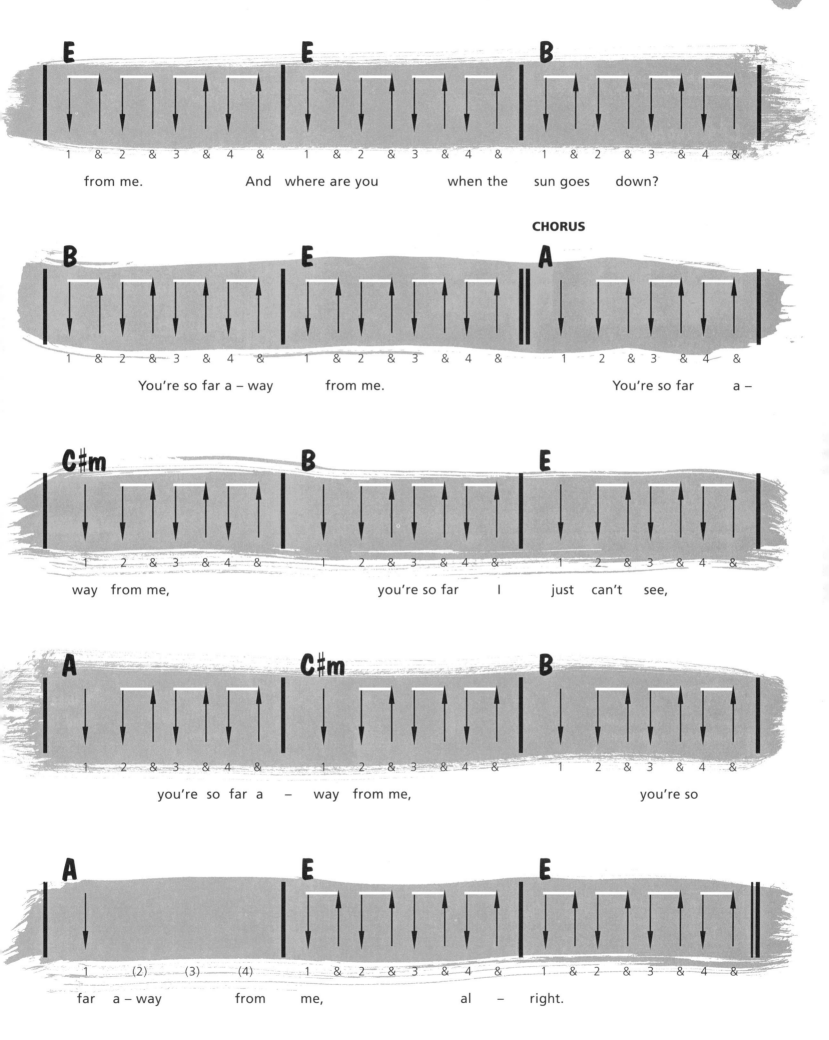

CHORUS

HALF THE WORLD AWAY
Words & Music by Noel Gallagher

D7 Chord
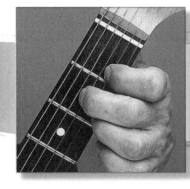

E7 Chord

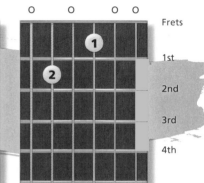

G7 Chord

Fm Chord
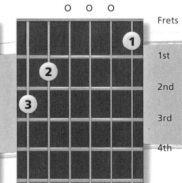
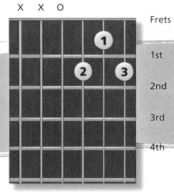

There are four new chords in this song: **D7, E7, G7, and Fm. The Fm chord is created by taking the Em you learned in "I Wanna Be Adored" and turning it into a barre chord.**

The relaxed, lazy strum of this song owes much to the use of the tied second offbeat, which you have played before.

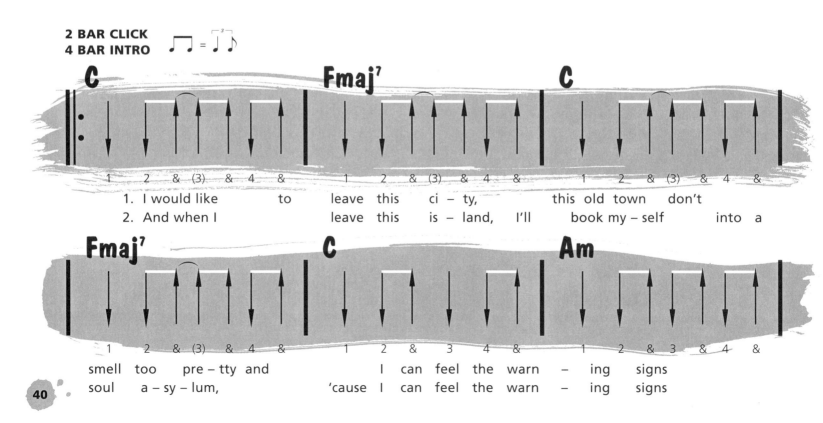

2 BAR CLICK
4 BAR INTRO

C   Fmaj⁷   C

1 2 & (3) & 4 &   1 2 & (3) & 4 &   1 2 & (3) & 4 &
1. I would like   to   leave this   ci — ty,   this old town   don't
2. And when I   leave this   is — land, I'll   book my — self   into a

Fmaj⁷   C   Am

1 2 & (3) & 4 &   1 2 & 3 4 &   1 2 & 3 & 4 &
smell too pre — tty and   I can feel the warn — ing signs
soul a — sy — lum,   'cause I can feel the warn — ing signs

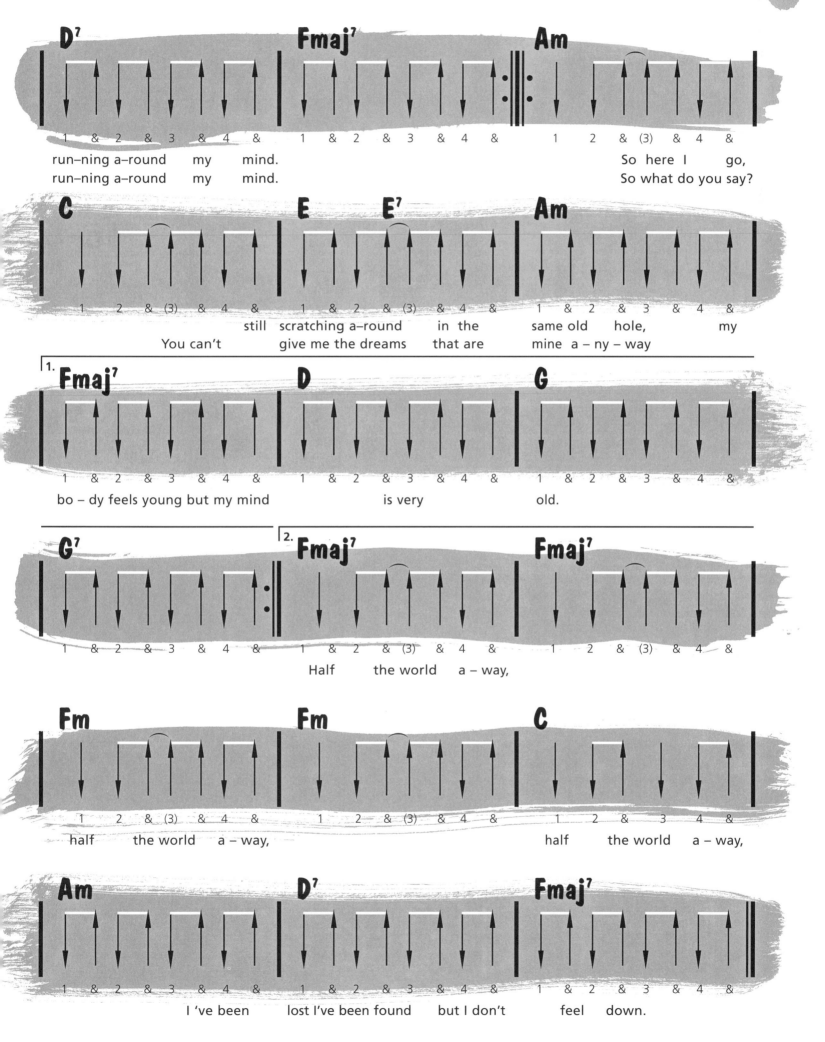

KODACHROME™
Words & Music by Paul Simon

A7 Chord

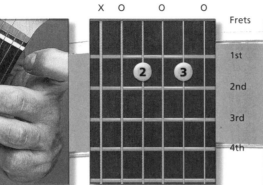

D/F♯ Chord

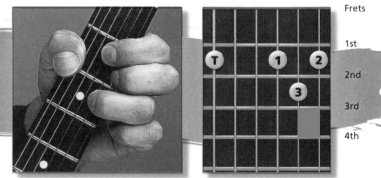

This song, by the great Paul Simon, reached No. 2 in the US charts in 1973. It is featured on the album *There Goes Rhymin' Simon.*

To play this song you will need three new chords: **A7, D/F♯,** and **Dm.**

D/F♯ is another inverted chord. Along with **G/B** (which you have already met), it is the most common inversion on the guitar. To play along with the original recording, capo up at the 9th fret.

The strumming is mostly straight 8ths, with some longer chords held through the beats in brackets. Watch out for measures 14 and 24, which only have three beats each instead of four. The numbers will help you count correctly.

So far with *The Complete Rock & Pop Guitar Player* you have learned 17 songs, over 20 chords, a number of strumming patterns, and you're starting to come to grips with barre chords. There are more great songs to play in **Parts 2** and **3,** and the chance to play some easy riffs and other single-note phrases.

* "Kodachrome™" is a registered trademark for color film

Dm Chord

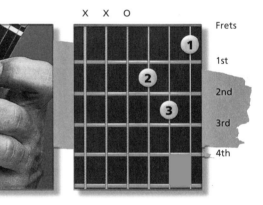

CAPO 9TH FRET
VERSE

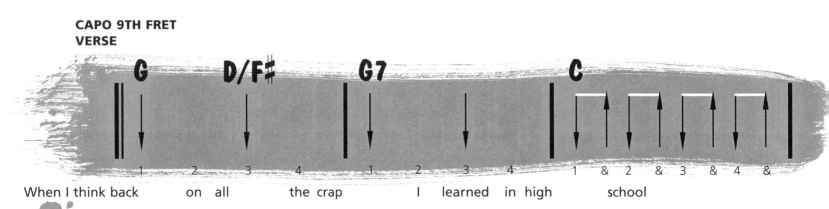

When I think back   on   all   the crap   I   learned   in   high   school

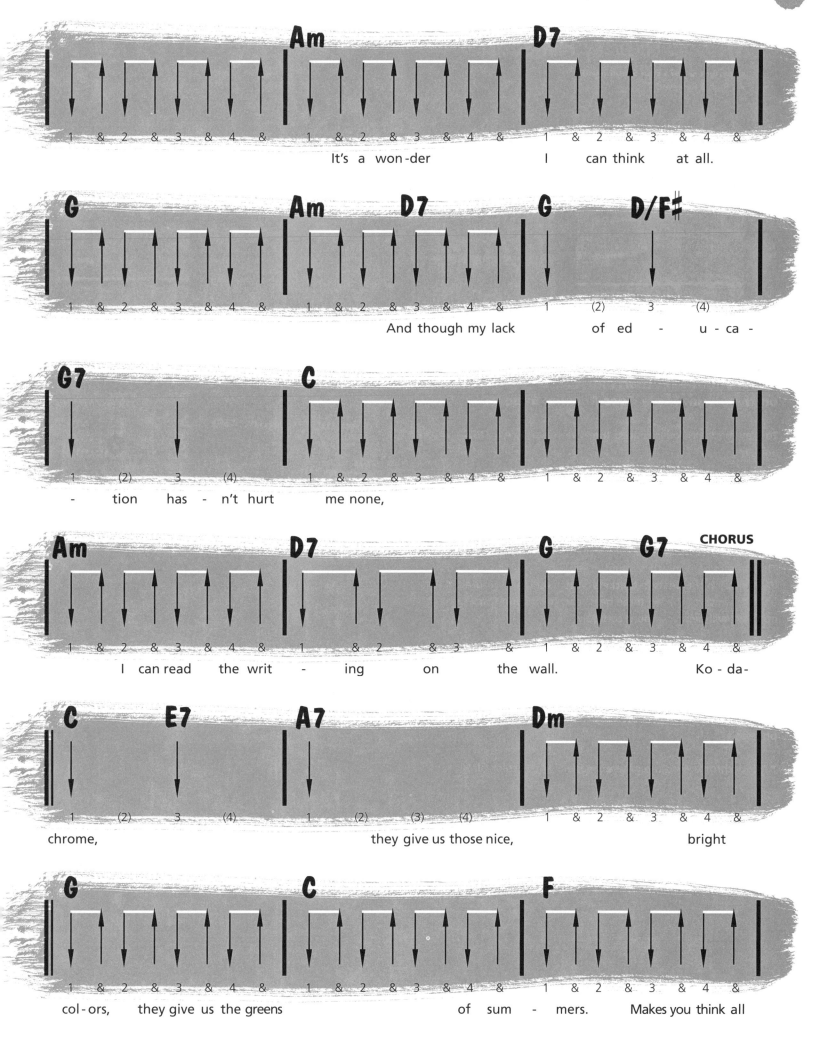

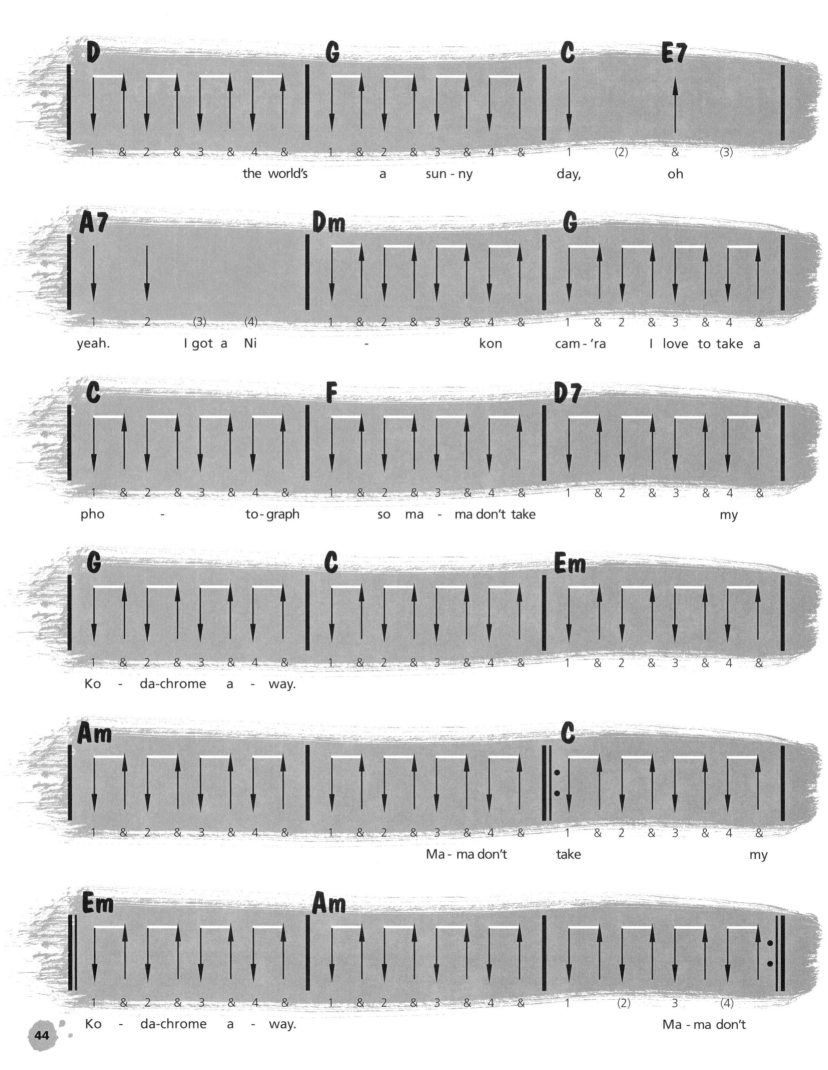

44

ADDITIONAL LYRICS

PAPERBACK WRITER

Paperback writer, Paperback writer…

Verse 1
Dear Sir or Madam,
will you read my book,
It took me years to write,
will you take a look?
It's based on a novel
by a man named Lear,
And I need a job,
So I want to be a paperback writer,
Paperback writer.

Verse 2
It's a dirty story of a dirty man,
And his clinging wife
doesn't understand.
His son is working for the Daily Mail,
It's a steady job,
But he wants to be a paperback writer,
Paperback writer.

Paperback writer, Paperback writer…

Verse 3
It's a thousand pages, give or take a few,
I'll be writing more in a week or two.
I can make it longer if you like the style,
I can change it round,
And I want to be a paperback writer,
Paperback writer.

Verse 4
If you really like it
you can have the rights,
It could make a million for you
overnight,
If you must return it,
you can send it here,
But I need a break
And I want to be a paperback writer,
Paperback writer.

Paperback writer, Paperback writer…

BRIMFUL OF ASHA

Verse 1
There's dancing behind movie scenes,
Behind the movie scenes Sadi Rani,
She's the one that keeps the dream alive
From the morning past the evening
To the end of the light.

Chorus
Brimful of Asha on the forty-five,
Well it's a brimful of Asha on the
forty-five.

Verse 2
And singing, illuminate the main streets
And the cinema aisles,
We don't care about no government
warnings
'Bout their promotion of the simple life
And the dams they're building.

Chorus

Bridge
Everybody needs a bosom for a pillow,
Everybody needs a bosom.
Mine's on the forty-five.

Verse 3
Mohamid Rufi. (Forty-five).
Lata Mangeskar. (Forty-five).
Solid state radio. (Forty-five).
Ferguson mono (Forty-five).
Bon Publeek (Forty-five).
Jacques Dutronc and the Bolan Boogie,
The Heavy Hitters and the chi-chi music,
All India radio.
Two-in-ones.
Argo records.
Trojan records.

Chorus

Bridge

Coda
Seventy-thousand piece orchestra set.
Everybody needs a bosom for a pillow,
Mine's on the r.p.m.

Brimful of Asha on the forty-five,
Well it's a brimful of Asha on the
forty-five.

Everybody needs a bosom for a pillow,
Everybody needs a bosom.
Mine's on the forty-five.

TWO TICKETS TO PARADISE

Verse 1
Got a surprise especially for you
Something that both of us have always
wanted to do
I've waited so long, I've waited so long
I've waited so long, I've waited so long.

Verse 2
I'm gonna take you on a trip so far from
here
I've got two tickets in my pocket
Now baby we're gonna disappear
I've waited so long, I've waited so long
I've waited so long, I've waited so long.

Chorus
I've got two tickets to paradise
Won't you pack your bags and we'll
leave tonight
I've got two tickets to paradise
I've got two tickets to paradise.

Repeat Verse 2

Chorus x 2

ROCK AROUND THE CLOCK

Intro
One, two, three o'clock,
four o'clock rock,
Five, six, seven o'clock,
eight o'clock rock,
Nine, ten, eleven o'clock,
twelve o'clock rock,
We're gonna rock around
the clock tonight!

Verse 1
Put your glad rags on and join me, Hon,
We'll have some fun when the clock
strikes one,
We're gonna rock around the
clock tonight,
We're gonna rock, rock, rock 'til
broad daylight,
We're gonna rock, gonna rock,
around the clock tonight.

Verse 2
When the clock strikes two,
and three and four,
If the band slows down
we'll ask for more,
We're gonna rock around the
clock tonight,
We're gonna rock, rock, rock 'til
broad daylight,
We're gonna rock, gonna rock,
around the clock tonight.

Verse 3
When the chimes ring five, six and
seven,
We'll be ridin' seventh heaven,
We're gonna rock around the clock
tonight,
We're gonna rock, rock, rock 'til
broad daylight,
We're gonna rock, gonna rock,
around the clock tonight.

Verse 4
When it's eight, nine, ten, eleven too,
I'll be goin' strong and so will you,
We're gonna rock around the
clock tonight,
We're gonna rock, rock, rock 'til
broad daylight,
We're gonna rock, gonna rock,
around the clock tonight.

Verse 5
When the clock strikes twelve,
we'll cool off, then
Start-a-rockin' round the
clock again,
We're gonna rock around the clock
tonight,
We're gonna rock, rock, rock 'til
broad daylight,
We're gonna rock, gonna rock,
around the clock tonight.

THAT'LL BE THE DAY

Chorus
Well, that'll be the day, when you say
goodbye
Yes that'll be the day, when you make
me cry
You say you're gonna leave, you know
it's a lie
'Cause that'll be the day when I die.

Verse 1
Well, you give me all your lovin' and
your turtle dovin'
All your hugs and kisses and your
money too
Well you know you love me baby
Until you tell me, maybe
That some day, well, I'll be through!

Chorus

Verse 2
When Cupid shot his dart, he shot it at
your heart
So if we ever part and I leave you
You say you told me and you told me
boldly
That some day, well, I'll be through.

Chorus

I WANNA BE ADORED

Verse 1
I don't need to sell my soul
He's already in me,
I don't need to sell my soul
He's already in me.

Chorus
I wanna be adored.
I wanna be adored.

Verse 2
I don't need to sell my soul
He's already in me,
I don't need to sell my soul
He's already in me.

Chorus

Bridge
Adored.
I wanna be adored.
You adore me, you adore me,
you adore me.
I wanna, I wanna, I wanna be adored.
I wanna, I wanna, I wanna be adored.
I wanna, I wanna, I wanna be adored.
I wanna, I wanna, I gotta be adored.

I wanna be adored.

STAND BY ME

Verse 1
When the night has come
And the land is dark
And the moon is the only light we'll see
No I won't be afraid
No I won't be afraid
Just as long as you stand, stand by me.

Chorus
So darling, darling, stand by me
Oh, stand by me.
Oh, stand, stand by me, stand by me.

Verse 2
If the sky that we look upon
Should tumble and fall
Or the mountain should crumble into
the sea
I won't cry, I won't cry
No I won't shed a tear
Just as long as you stand, stand by me.

Chorus

CATHY'S CLOWN

Chorus
Don't want your love anymore,
Don't want your kisses back for sure.
I die each time I hear this sound:
Here he comes—that's Cathy's clown.

Verse 1
I've gotta stand tall,
You know a man can't crawl
But when he knows you're telling lies
And he hears them passing by
Then he's not a man at all.

Chorus

Verse 2
When you see me shed a tear
And you know that it's sincere,
But wouldn't you think it's kinda sad
That you're treating me so bad
Or do you even care?

Chorus

COMMON PEOPLE

Verse 1
She came from Greece, she had a thirst for knowledge,
She studied sculpture at St. Martin's College,
That's where I caught her eye.
She told me that her Dad was loaded,
I said, "In that case I'll have rum and Coca-Cola,"
She said, "Fine."
And then in thirty seconds time she said,

Chorus
"I want to live like common people,
I want to do whatever common people do,
Want to sleep with common people,
I want to sleep with common people
Like you."
Well, what else could I do?
I said, "I'll ... I'll see what I can do."

Verse 2
I took her to a supermarket,
I don't know why but I had to start it somewhere, so it started there.

I said, "Pretend you've got no money,"
She just laughed and said, "Oh, you're so funny," I said, "Yeah?"
(Well I can't see anyone else smiling in here),
Are you sure?

Chorus
"You want to live like common people,
You want to see whatever common people see,
You want to sleep with common people,
You want to sleep with common people like me."

Verse 3
Rent a flat above a shop, cut your hair and get a job,
Smoke some fags and play some pool,
pretend you never went to school,
But still you'll never get it right 'cause when you're laid in bed at night
Watching 'roaches climb the wall,
If you called your Dad he could stop it all, yeah.

Chorus
You'll never live like common people,
You'll never do whatever common people do;
You'll never fail like common people,
You'll never watch your life slide out of view
And then dance and drink and screw
Because there's nothing else to do.

Chorus
Sing along with the common people,
Sing along and it might just get you through.
Laugh along with the common people,
Laugh along even though they're laughing at you
And the stupid things that you do,
Because you think that poor is cool.

Bridge
Like a dog lying in the corner,
They will bite you and never warn you,
Look out, they'll tear your insides out,
'Cause everybody hates a tourist,
Especially one who thinks it's all such a laugh,
And the chip stains and grease will come out in the bath.
You will never understand how it feels to live your life
With no meaning or control and nowhere left to go.
You are amazed that they exist
And they burn so bright whilst you can only wonder why.

Verse 4
Rent a flat above a shop, cut your hair and get a job,
Smoke some fags and play some pool,
pretend you never went to school,
But still you'll never get it right 'cause when you're laid in bed at night
Watching 'roaches climb the wall,
If you called your Dad he could stop it all, yeah.

Chorus
You'll never live like common people,
You'll never do whatever common people do,
You'll never fail like common people,
You'll never watch your life slide out of view
And then dance and drink and screw
Because there's nothing else to do.

Want to live with common people like you.

ALL ALONG THE WATCHTOWER

Verse 1
"There must be some way out of here,"
Said the joker to the thief,
"There's too much confusion,
I can't get no relief.
Business men, they drink my wine,
Ploughmen dig my earth,
None of them along the line
Know what any of it is worth."

Verse 2
"No reason to get excited,"
The thief he kindly spoke,
"There are many here among us
Who feel that life is but a joke.
But you and I we've been through that,
And this is not our fate,
So let us not talk falsely now,
The hour is getting late."

Verse 3
All along the watchtower
Princes kept the view
While other women came and went,
Barefoot servants, too.
Outside in the distance
A wildcat did growl,
Two riders were approaching,
The wind began to howl.

NO WOMAN, NO CRY

Chorus
No woman, no cry, no woman, no cry.
No woman, no cry, no woman, no cry.

Verse 1
Say, say, said I remember
when we used to sit
In the government yard in Trenchtown,
Oba-observing the hypocrites
As they would mingle with the good
people we meet.
Good friends we have had,
oh good friends we've lost
Along the way.
In this bright future you can't forget
your past,
So dry your tears, I say, and...

Chorus

Verse 2
Said, said, said I remember
when we used to sit
In the government yard in Trenchtown,
And then Georgie would make the fire
light
As it was log wood burning through the
night.
Then we would cook corn meal porridge
Of which I'll share with you.
My feet is my only carriage
So I've got to push on through,
But while I'm gone I mean...

Bridge
Everything's gonna be alright,
Everything's gonna be alright.

Chorus
No woman, no cry, no no woman, no
woman, no cry.
Oh little sister, don't shed no tears,
No woman, no cry.

Verse 3
Said, said, said I remember
when we used to sit
In the government yard in Trenchtown,
And then Georgie would make
the fire light
As it was log wood burning through
the night.
Then we would cook corn meal porridge
Of which I'll share with you.
My feet is my only carriage
So I've got to push on through,
But while I'm gone I mean ...

Chorus
No woman, no cry, no woman, no cry.
Oh c'mon little darlin', say don't shed no
tears,
No woman, no cry.

DANCE AWAY

Verse 1
Yesterday, well it seemed so cool
When I walked you home, kissed
goodnight
I said "It's love," you said "Alright"
It's funny how I could never cry
Until tonight and you pass by
Hand in hand with another guy
You're dressed to kill and guess who's
dying?

Chorus
Dance away the heartaches,
dance away the tears
Dance away the heartaches,
dance away the tears
Dance away

Verse 2
Loneliness is a crowded room
Full of open hearts, turned to stone
All together, all alone.
All at once my whole world had changed
Now I'm in the dark, off the wall
Let the strobe light up them all
I close my eyes and dance till dawn

Chorus

Verse 3
Now I know I must walk the line
Until I find an open door
Off the street on to the floor
There was I many times a fool
I hope and pray but not too much
Out of reach is out of touch
All the way is far enough

Chorus

Outro
Dance away, dance away, dance away
Dance away the heartaches,
dance away the tears
Dance away the heartaches,
dance away the tears
Dance away the heartaches,
dance away the tears
Dance away the heartaches,
dance away the tears.

THAT'S ENTERTAINMENT

Verse 1
A police car and a screaming siren,
Pneumatic drill and ripped up concrete;
A baby wailing, a stray dog howling,
The screech of brakes and lamplight
blinking:
That's entertainment,
that's entertainment.

Verse 2
A smash of glass and the rumble
of boots,
An electric train and a ripped-up phone
booth,
Paint-splattered walls and the cry of
a tom-cat,
Lights going out, and a kick in the balls.
That's entertainment,
that's entertainment.

Verse 3
Days of speed and slow-time Mondays,
Pissing down with rain on a boring
Wednesday;
Watching the news and not eating
your tea,
A freezing cold flat and damp on
the walls.
I say, that's entertainment,
that's entertainment.

Verse 4
Waking up at 6:00 a.m. on a cold warm
morning,
Opening the windows and breathing
in petrol;
An amateur band rehearsing in
a nearby yard,
Watching the telly and thinking 'bout
your holidays.
That's entertainment,
that's entertainment.

Verse 5
Waking up from bad dreams and
smoking cigarettes,
Cuddling a warm girl and smelling
stale perfume;
A hot summer's day and sticky black
tarmac,
Feeding ducks in the park and wishing
you were far away.
That's entertainment,
that's entertainment.

Verse 6
Two lovers kissing amongst the scream
of midnight,
Two lovers missing the tranquility of
solitude;
Getting a cab and travelling on buses,
Reading the graffiti about slashed seat
affairs.
I said, that's entertainment,
that's entertainment.

THE TIDE IS HIGH

Chorus
The tide is high and I'm holding on
I'm gonna be your number one.

Bridge
I'm not the kinda girl
Who gives up just like that
Oh, no.

Verse 1
It's not the things you do
That tease and hurt me bad
But it's the way you do the things
You do to me.

Bridge

Chorus

Tag
Number one
Number one

Verse 2
Every girl wants you to be her man
But I'll wait, my dear, till it's my turn.

Bridge

Chorus

Tag

Repeat Verse 2

Bridge

Chorus

Tag x 2

Chorus x 4

SO FAR AWAY

Verse 1
Here I am again in this mean old town
And you're so far away from me,
And where are you when the sun goes
down?
You're so far away from me.

Chorus
So far away from me,
So far I just can't see,
So far away from me,
You're so far away from me.

Verse 2
I'm tired of being in love and being all
alone
When you're so far away from me.
I'm tired of making out on the
telephone
'Cause you're so far away from me.

Chorus

Verse 3
I get so tired when I have to explain
When you're so far away from me.
See you've been in the sun and I've been
in the rain
And you're so far away from me.

Chorus

You're so far away from me

HALF THE WORLD AWAY

Verse 1
I would like to leave this city,
This old town don't smell too pretty,
And I can feel the warning signs
Running around my mind.
And when I leave this island
I'll book myself into a soul asylum
'Cause I can feel the warning signs
Running around my mind.

Prechorus
So here I go,
Still scratching around in the same
old hole,
My body is young but my mind feels
very old.

Chorus
So what do you say?
You can't give me the dreams that are
mine anyway.
Half the world away, half the world
away,
Half the world away:
I've been lost I've been found but
I don't feel down.

Verse 2
And when I leave this planet
You know I'd stay
but I just can't stand it,
And I can feel the warning signs
Running around my mind.
And if I could leave this spirit
I'd find me a hole and I'd live in it
And I can feel the warning signs
Running around my mind.

Prechorus
Here I go I'm still scratching around in
the same old hole,
My body feels young but my mind is
very old.

Chorus
No, I don't feel down.

KODACHROME™

Verse 1
When I think back on all the crap
I learned in high school
It's a wonder I can think at all
And though my lack of education
Hasn't hurt me none
I can read the writing on the wall.

Chorus
Kodachrome
They give us those nice, bright colors
They give us the greens of summers
Makes you think all the world's a sunny
day, oh yeah
I got a Nikon camera
I love to take a photograph
So mama don't take my Kodachrome
away.

Verse 2
If you took all the girls I knew
When I was single
And brought them all together for one
night
I know they'd never match my sweet
imagination
And everything looks worse in black and
white.

Chorus

(*"KODACHROME" is a registered
trademark for color film)

The Complete Rock & Pop Guitar Player
Part 2

INTRODUCTION

This is the second part in *The Complete Rock & Pop Guitar Player* course. As before, all the songs you will learn to play have been big hits for well-known artists.

By following strum patterns in **Part 1** you will already be accustomed to learning songs in this format. **Part 2** features more strumming patterns and some new chords. But it has an extra feature. Some of the songs have short musical examples written in standard notation and guitar-friendly TAB.

Full lyrics are included on pages 88–93.
The songs have been graded; each one introduces new chords, strum patterns or necessary revision of what you have already learned.

As with all parts of this course, it is suitable for use with or without a teacher.

BLUE SUEDE SHOES
Words & Music by Carl Lee Perkins

A9 Chord   ## D9 Chord

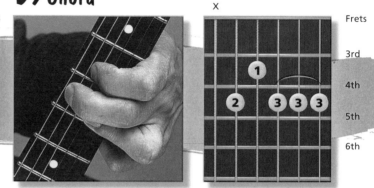

Elvis Presley

Blue Suede Shoes" was an early hit for Elvis in 1956. It's another example of a rock'n'roll 12-bar but with some new chord substitutions. In Part 1 you saw how a 12-bar could be played with A, D, and E.

You also learned the shapes for **D7** and **E7,** which can be substituted for the simple **D** or **E major** to add a bit more "color." The next step is to try the **9th** chord.

These five-note chords are extensions of 7ths like **D7,** **C7,** and **B7,** and are often heard in rock'n'roll and blues music. To get **E9** simply move the **D9** shape up **two frets.**

Notice how on the intro you only strum intermittently in the places indicated. The steady strum does not begin until the **D9** and even so it has more "spaces" in it than some of the songs you have learned.

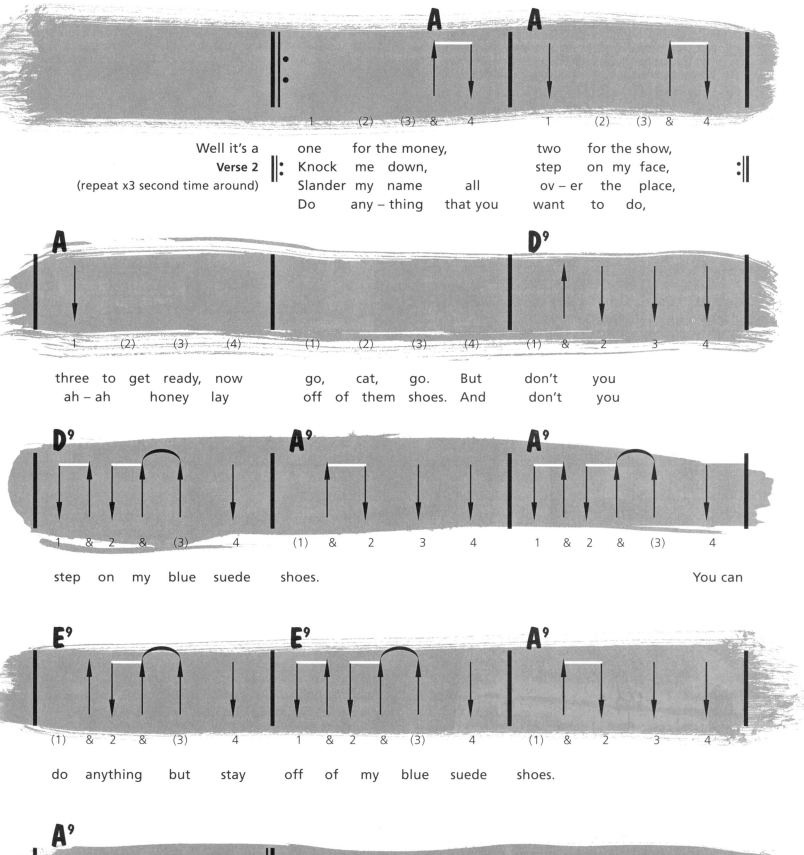

Well it's a   one   for the money,   two   for the show,

Verse 2   Knock   me down,   step   on my face,

(repeat x3 second time around)   Slander my name all   ov – er the place,

Do   any – thing that you   want   to do,

three to get ready, now   go,   cat,   go. But   don't   you

ah – ah honey lay   off of them shoes. And   don't   you

step on my blue suede   shoes.   You can

do anything but stay   off of my blue suede shoes.

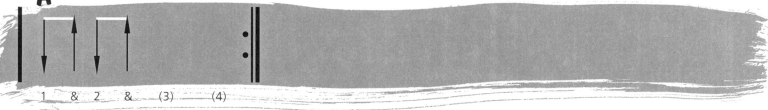

2. Well you can

DRIFTWOOD
Words & Music by Francis Healy

This ambient ballad by Travis gets part of its sound from the fact that the acoustic guitar on the original is played with a capo at the 7th fret. So to play along with the CD demonstration you will need to do the same.

This song requires two new chords: **Asus4** and **G6**—both easy shapes!

In the **Asus4** chord one of the original three notes of **A major** has been replaced by another, the fourth of the scale. "**Sus**" is short for "**suspended.**" You can find out more about the way chords are made in **Part 3.** For the moment all you need to know is that this **Asus4** is neither major nor minor. Notice it has a tense quality.

Fran Healy (Travis)

Asus4 Chord

G6 Chord

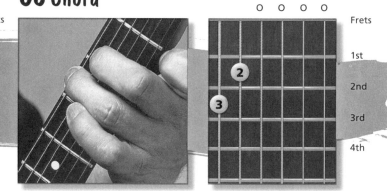

For the chorus of "**Driftwood**" you can try a continuous 16th-note strum. This means going down and up twice on each beat, instead of once for 8ths. It is more usual to find 16ths used occasionally because they get quite tiring to play, and also because they only really work at slow to medium speeds. If you wish, you can play 16ths throughout the whole song. To improve the sound of a 16th-note strum use a thin pick and brush the strings lightly up and down.

2 BAR CLICK + 4 BAR INTRO

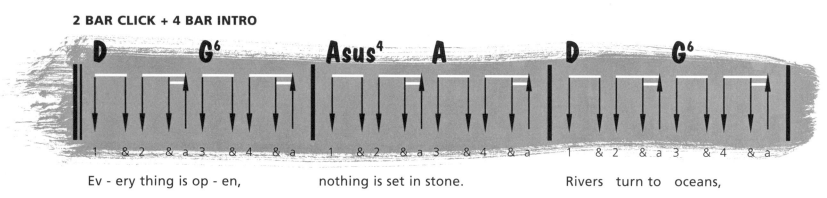

Ev - ery thing is op - en,   nothing is set in stone.   Rivers turn to oceans,

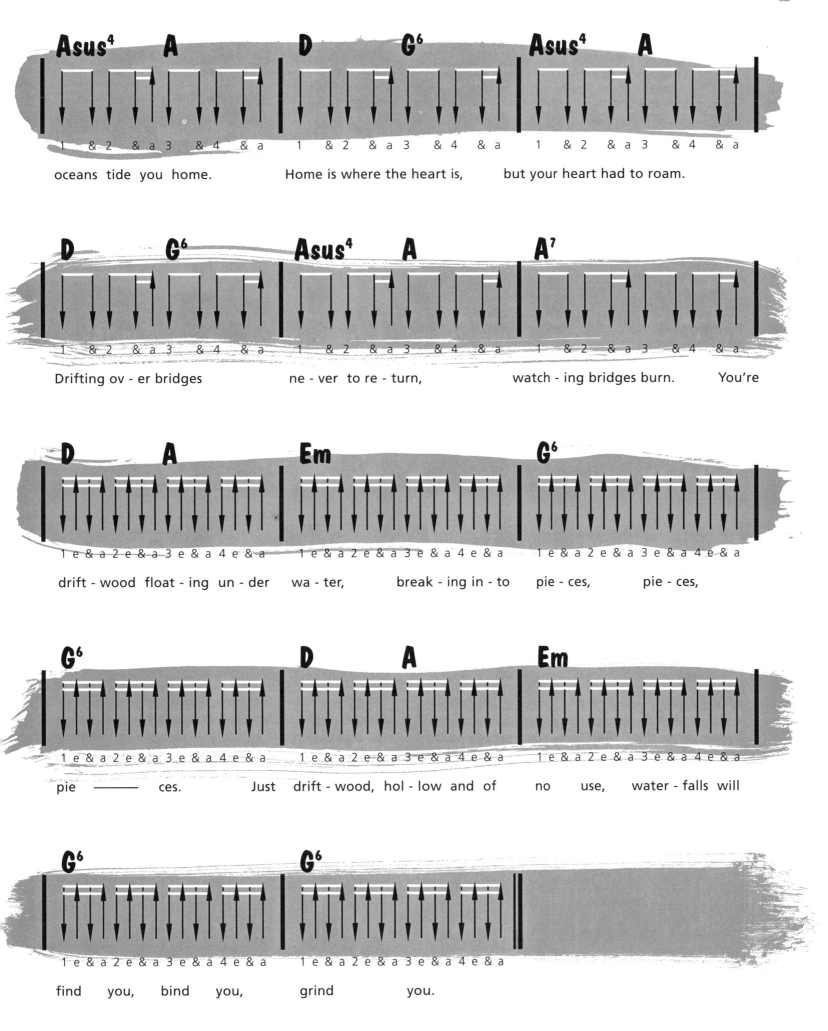

SAIL AWAY
Words & Music by David Gray

Bmadd¹¹ Chord

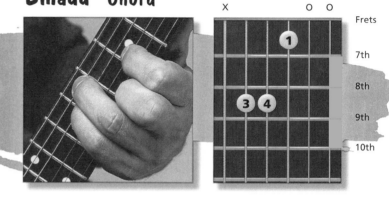

This hit for David Gray introduces a new idea you can apply to the chord shapes you have learned.

These two chords are derived from the **F#m** chord shape you met in **Part 1**. What has happened is that the barre has been taken off, the first finger has gone to the 3rd string and the 6th string is not played.

This song features a new, complicated off-beat strumming pattern for you to learn. The best way to do this is to listen to the demonstration track and try and "feel" the rhythm. The other way to learn it is by slowing it right down and counting. Here's how it should go:

F#m11 Chord

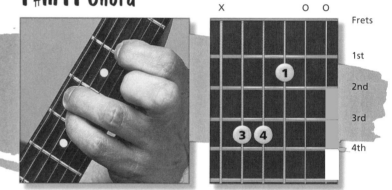

Only count, or play, the bold notes. It looks complicated, but slow it right down and you should get the feel of the rhythm. Then, gradually speed it up.

If you can't manage this you can always play any of the other 4/4 rhythm patterns you've learned. Just try and pick one that would fit the feel of this song.

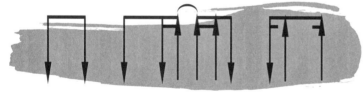

1 (e) **& (a) 2** (e) **& a** (3) **e & (a) 4** e **(&) a**

CAPO 1ST FRET
1 BAR CLICK + 4 BAR INTRO

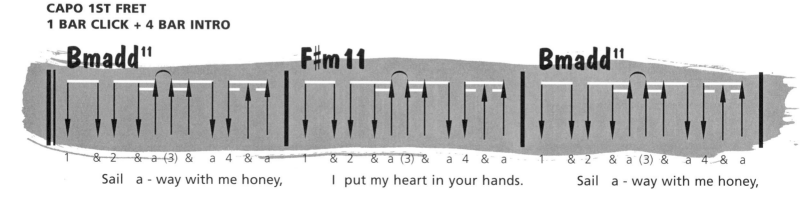

Bmadd¹¹   **F#m11**   **Bmadd¹¹**

1   & 2   & a (3) & a 4 & a   1   & 2   & a (3) & a 4 & a   1   & 2   & a (3) & a 4 & a

Sail a - way with me honey,   I put my heart in your hands.   Sail a - way with me honey,

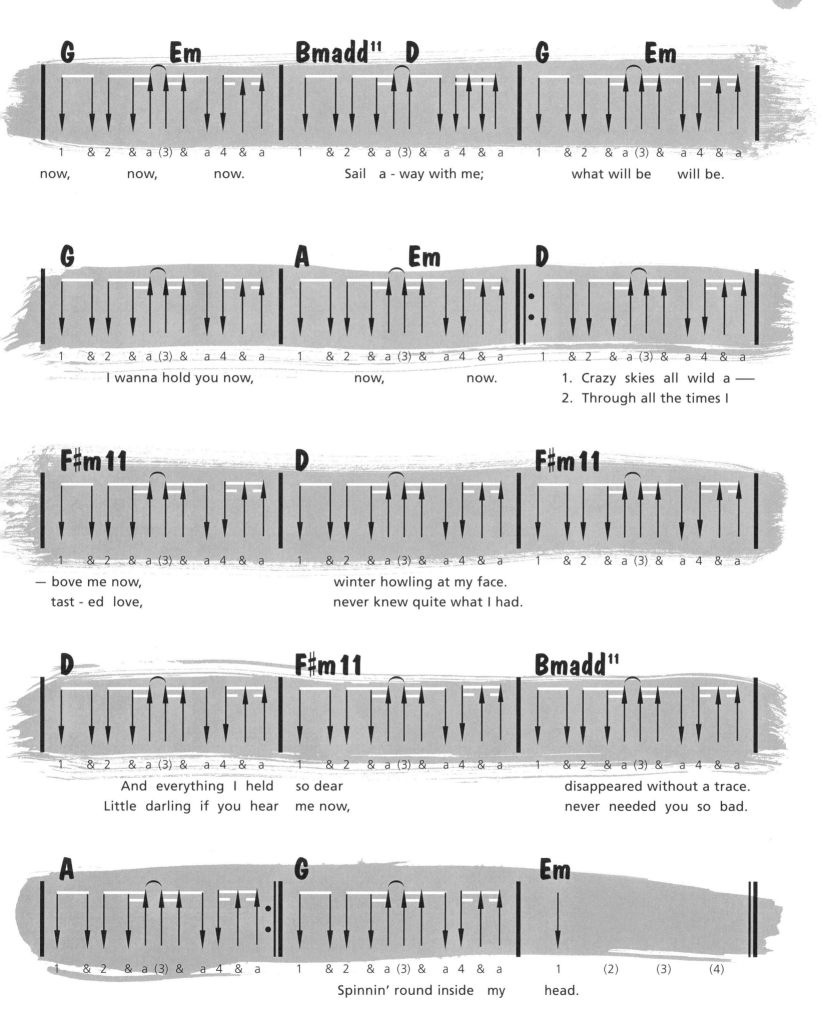

WILD WOOD
Words & Music by Paul Weller, Per Magnusson & David Krueger

F#m/B Chord

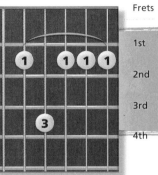

Em7 Chord

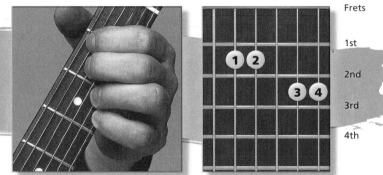

This UK hit by Paul Weller has a relaxed acoustic feel that is quite easy to reproduce. There are three new chord shapes for you.

The **Em7** is a less common shape for this chord than the **Em7** you learned in **Part 1,** but makes more sense harmonically for this song. The **C9** helps to give "**Wild Wood**" its slightly jazzy quality.

C9 Chord

The **Bm** chord is the standard **Bm barre** shape and can be played by using the **C#m** shape in **Part 1** moved down two frets.

With the strumming, watch out for the quick up and down that comes on the last beat of the bar.

Paul Weller

1 BAR CLICK + 4 BAR INTRO

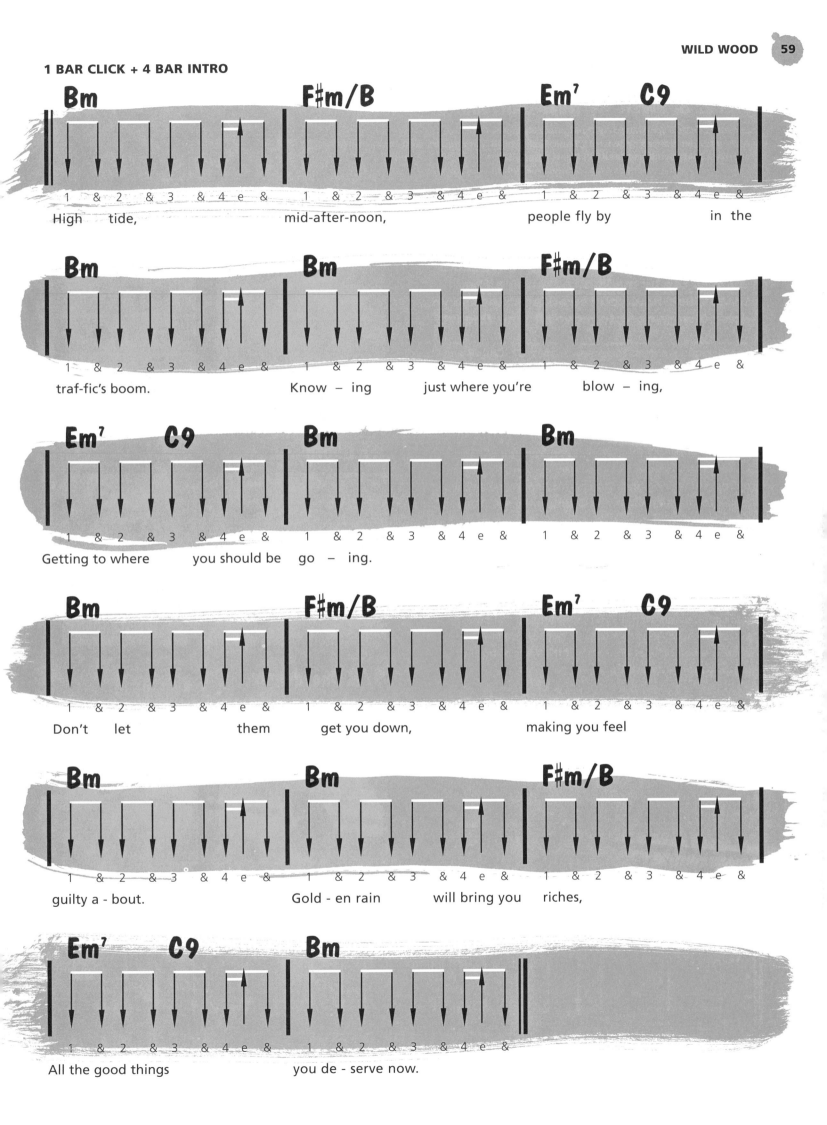

Bm · F#m/B · Em7 · C9

1 & 2 & 3 & 4 e & | 1 & 2 & 3 & 4 e & | 1 & 2 & 3 & 4 e &

High tide, mid-after-noon, people fly by in the

Bm · Bm · F#m/B

1 & 2 & 3 & 4 e & | 1 & 2 & 3 & 4 e & | 1 & 2 & 3 & 4 e &

traf-fic's boom. Know – ing just where you're blow – ing,

Em7 · C9 · Bm · Bm

1 & 2 & 3 & 4 e & | 1 & 2 & 3 & 4 e & | 1 & 2 & 3 & 4 e &

Getting to where you should be go – ing.

Bm · F#m/B · Em7 · C9

1 & 2 & 3 & 4 e & | 1 & 2 & 3 & 4 e & | 1 & 2 & 3 & 4 e &

Don't let them get you down, making you feel

Bm · Bm · F#m/B

1 & 2 & 3 & 4 e & | 1 & 2 & 3 & 4 e & | 1 & 2 & 3 & 4 e &

guilty a - bout. Gold - en rain will bring you riches,

Em7 · C9 · Bm

1 & 2 & 3 & 4 e & | 1 & 2 & 3 & 4 e &

All the good things you de - serve now.

ROLL WITH IT
Words & Music by Noel Gallagher

Roll With It" was one of several hit singles taken from Oasis' huge album *(What's The Story) Morning Glory?* (1995). It is a good example of how effective chord changes can be made by adapting a few shapes, and how you can adapt shapes so you don't always need to move all your fingers.

For this song we need three new shapes: **C7**, **Cadd9** and **G/B**, which are pretty simple, straightforward open chords. The 7th chords give the intro a hard, no-nonsense rock sound.

You may remember the **G/B** inversion from **Part 1**. This variation requires some extra fingers to sound the new notes on top. This voicing gives the chord a brighter quality, and makes the transition from the **Cadd9** to the **Am** sound smoother.

Most of the strumming in "Roll With It" is straight 8ths, with examples of omitted offbeat strums from time to time.

These little variations help to make your strumming more interesting than if you played 8ths all the time. Letting a chord ring for a beat or two, or coming back in on an offbeat are some of the ways of making rhythms more interesting.

Cadd9 Chord

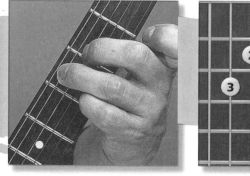
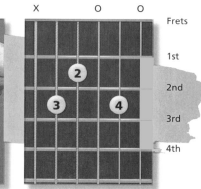

C7 Chord

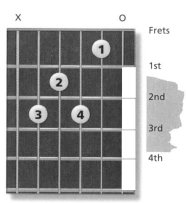

G/B Chord

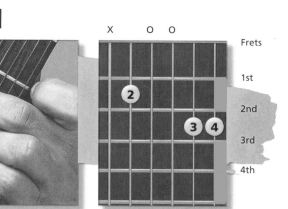

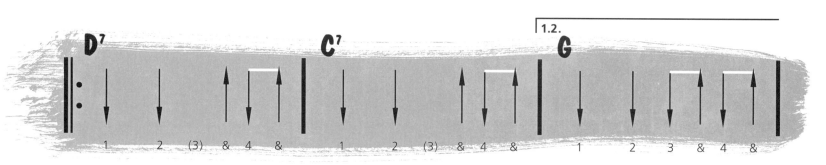

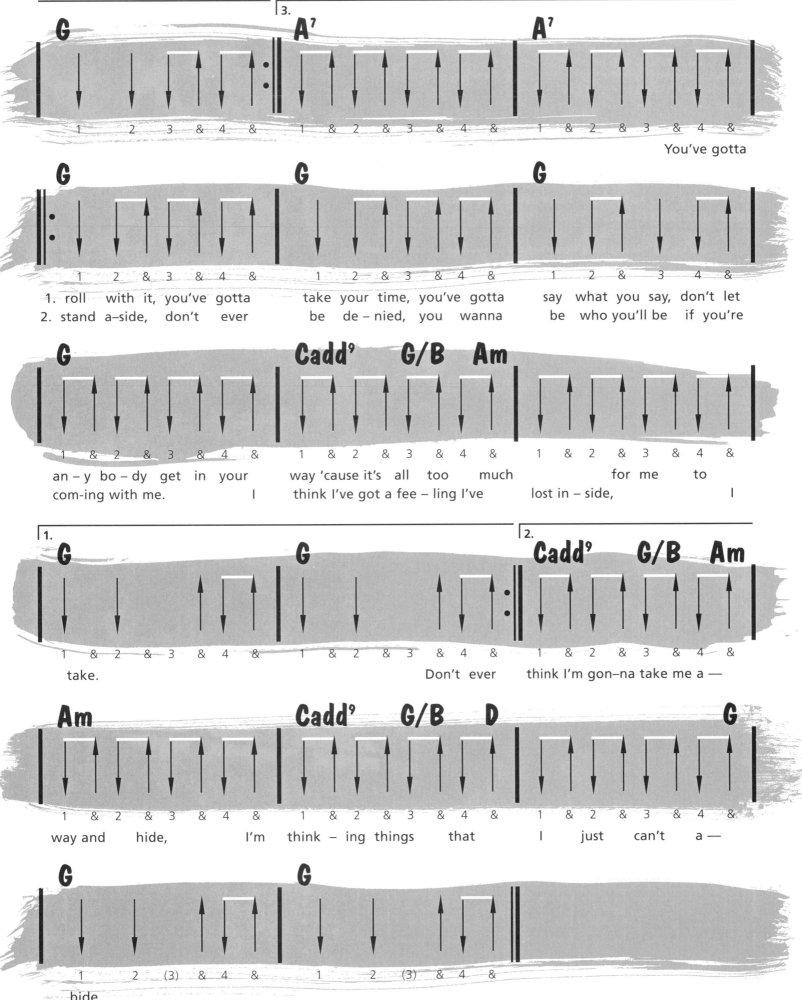

20TH CENTURY BOY
Words & Music by Marc Bolan

This classic slice of glam rock was a hit for T.Rex first in 1973, then in 1991 after use on a Levi's commercial, and also featured on the soundtrack of the film *Billy Elliot*. "20th Century Boy" uses the chords E, A, and B—all of which you have played before.

The strum for **"20th Century Boy"** is mostly 8ths. Watch out for the 8th/16th/16th figure on the last beat of bar 2, which can also be found elsewhere in the song. You can also try learning the song's famous riff (see TAB below).

The arrow indicates that the 2nd fret (**F♯**) on the bottom **E** string is bent a half step, and is called a half-step bend. To play this, push the string upwards quickly after striking the note.

Marc Bolan (T.Rex)

Here is the song's opening guitar riff:

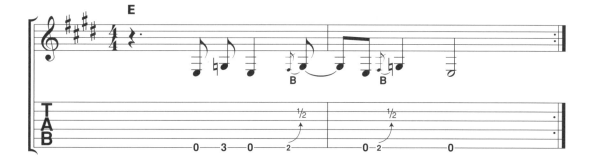

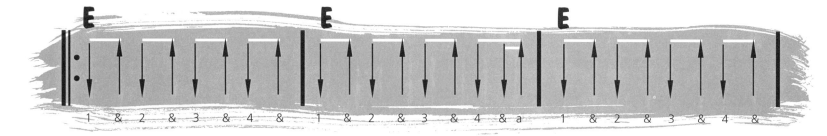

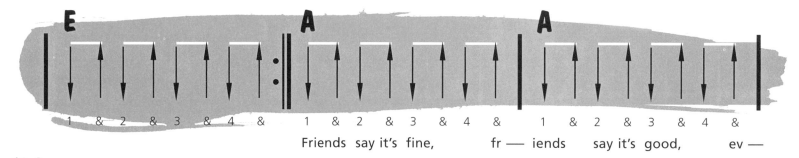

Friends say it's fine,   fr — iends   say it's good,   ev —

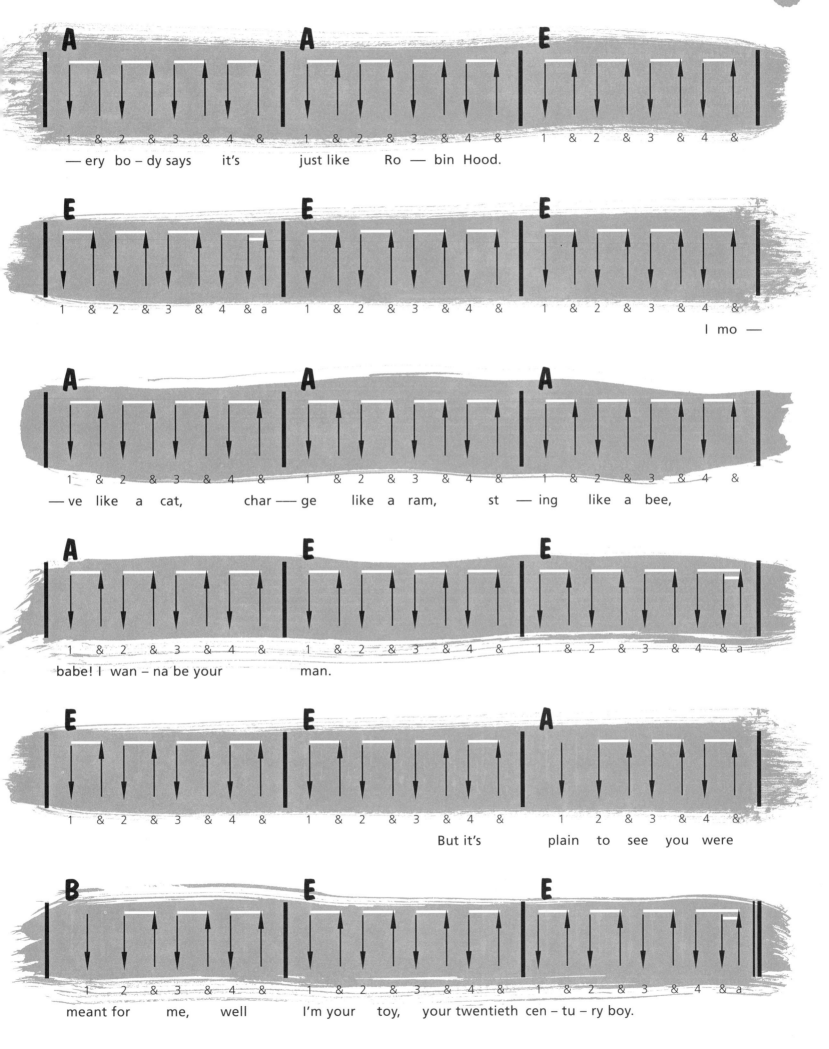

SHE LOVES YOU
Words & Music by John Lennon & Paul McCartney

This great example of the early "Fab Four" features the chords G, Em, Bm, D, D7 and A, all of which you know. The Cm can be played by taking the Bm from "Wild Wood" and moving it up one fret.

"She Loves You" has two famous guitar fills. Here they are:

GUITAR FILL 1

GUITAR FILL 2

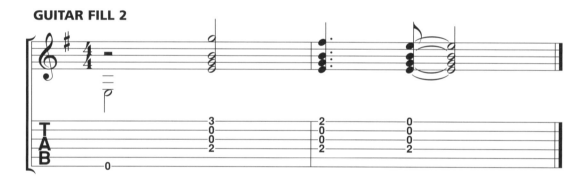

CAPO 1ST FRET

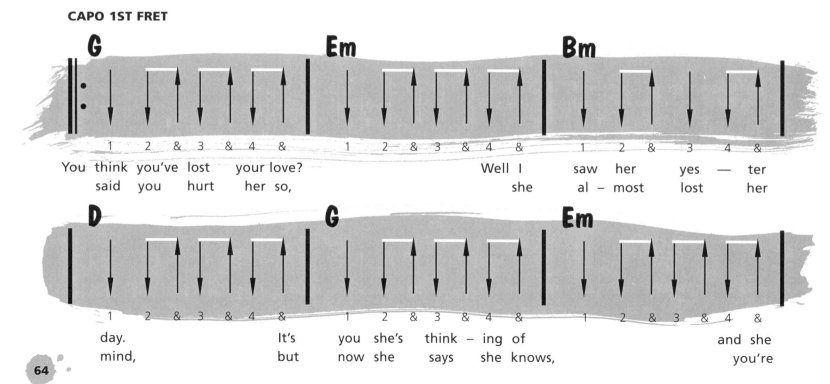

G

1	2	&	3	&	4	&

You think you've lost your love?
said you hurt her so,

Em

1	2	&	3	&	4	&

Bm

1	2	&	3	4	&

Well I saw her yes — ter
she al – most lost her

D

1	2	&	3	&	4	&

day.
mind,

G

1	2	&	3	&	4	&

It's you she's think – ing of
but now she says she knows,

Em

1	2	&	3	&	4	&

and she
you're

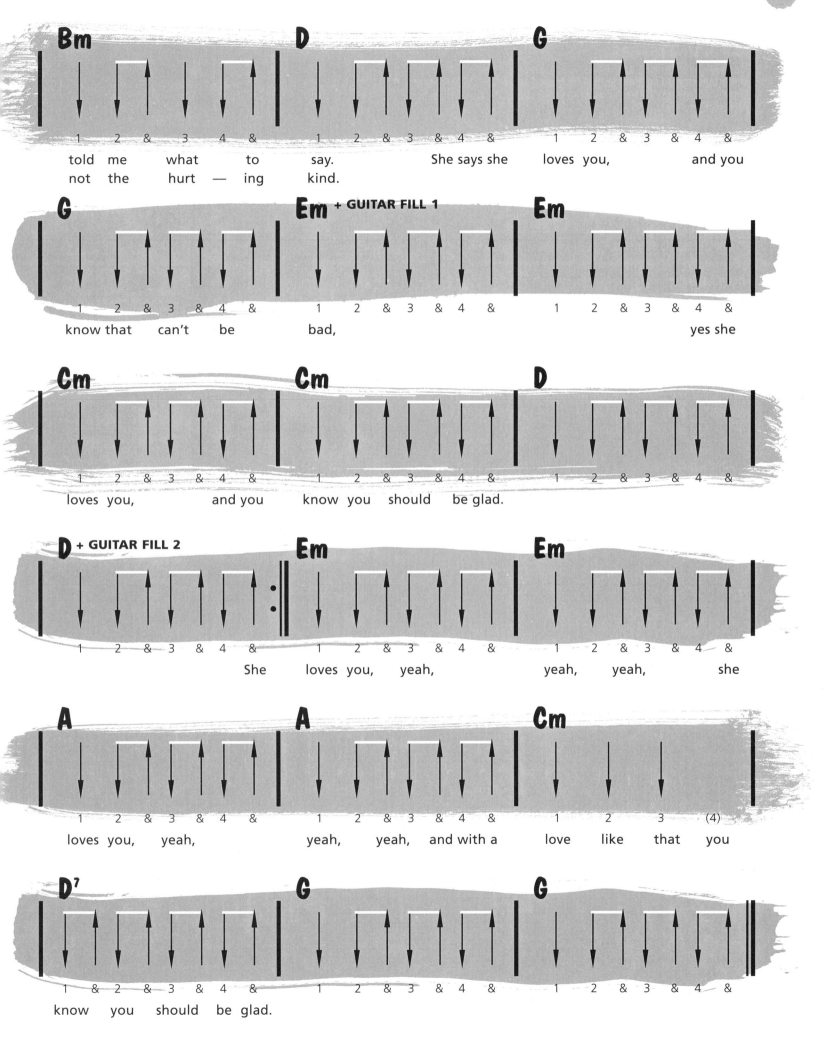

Bm   **D**   **G**

1 2 & 3 4 &   1 2 & 3 & 4 &   1 2 & 3 & 4 &

told me what to say. She says she loves you, and you
not the hurt — ing kind.

G   **Em** + GUITAR FILL 1   **Em**

1 2 & 3 & 4 &   1 2 & 3 & 4 &   1 2 & 3 & 4 &

know that can't be bad, yes she

Cm   **Cm**   **D**

1 2 & 3 & 4 &   1 2 & 3 & 4 &   1 2 & 3 & 4 &

loves you, and you know you should be glad.

D + GUITAR FILL 2   **Em**   **Em**

1 2 & 3 & 4 &   1 2 & 3 & 4 &   1 2 & 3 & 4 &

She loves you, yeah, yeah, yeah, she

A   **A**   **Cm**

1 2 & 3 & 4 &   1 2 & 3 & 4 &   1 2 3 (4)

loves you, yeah, yeah, yeah, and with a love like that you

D⁷   **G**   **G**

1 & 2 & 3 & 4 &   1 2 & 3 & 4 &   1 2 & 3 & 4 &

know you should be glad.

FATHER AND SON

By Cat Stevens

This famous song by Cat Steven has been covered by many bands and artists and is featured on his multi-platinum album *Tea For The Tillerman.*

The strumming pattern is mostly 1 2 &-a 3 4 &-a, so count off slowly to fit in the quick strums. Watch the counting in the second ending, where there are five beats in the measure, and three measures before the end, where there are only three beats.

There are two new chords: **Bm7** and **Cmaj7**.

Cmaj7 can also be played by holding down a **C** chord and lifting your 1st finger off the 2nd string. However this barre version sounds better here and makes the change to **Bm7** easier (both barred and the third finger is a guide finger).

Bm7 Chord

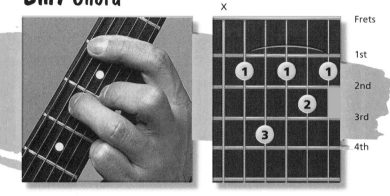

Cmaj7 Chord

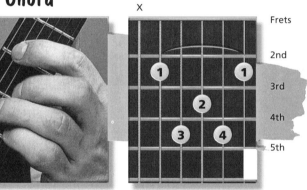

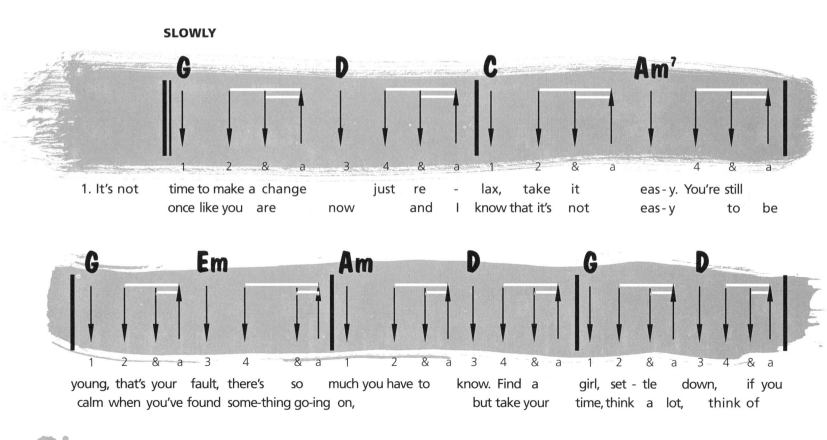

SLOWLY

G   **D**   **C**   **Am⁷**

1   2   &   a   3   4   &   a   1   2   &   a   4   &   a

1. It's not   time to make a change   just re - lax, take it   eas - y. You're still
     once like you are   now   and I know that it's not   eas - y   to be

G   **Em**   **Am**   **D**   **G**   **D**

1   2   &   a   3   4   &   a   1   2   &   a   3   4   &   a   1   2   &   a   3   4   &   a

young, that's your fault, there's   so   much you have to   know. Find a   girl, set - tle   down,   if you
calm when you've found some-thing go-ing on,   but take your   time, think a lot,   think of

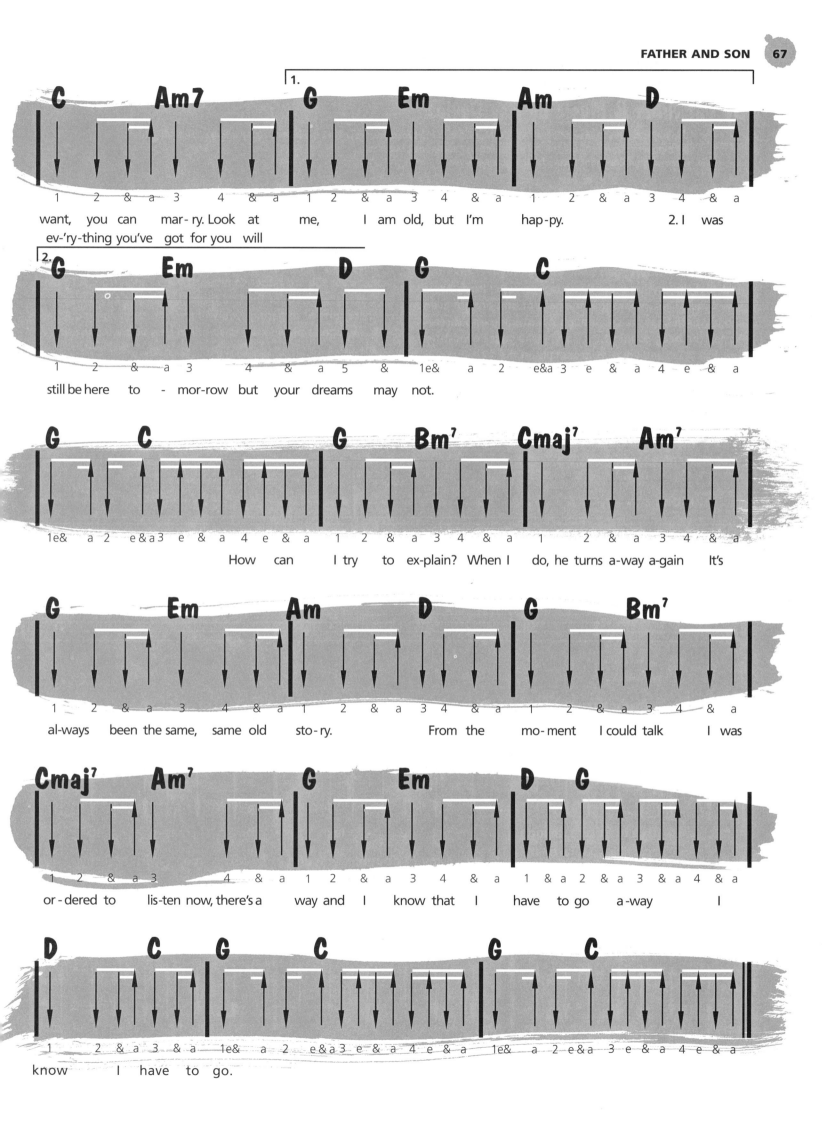

SUNNY AFTERNOON
Words & Music by Ray Davies

You know all the chords to be able to play this summer hit from the Kinks.

"Sunny Afternoon" gets some of its jaunty feel from the fact that the rhythm is lightly swung. As with "Rock Around The Clock," this means that the pairs of 8ths are not even in length. Each beat feels as though it is dividing into three. So tap the beat, count "1,2,3," and make your down strum last for "1,2," and your up strum falls on the "3."

When you are working out how to do a chord change always look to see if there is a guide finger. This is a finger that either moves up or down the same string or doesn't move at all. So if you change from **C** to **F (full barre)** there is no need for the 3rd finger to move. If you change from **A** to **Dm** there is no need for the 2nd finger to move. If you notice these sorts of fingerings you will find chord changing quicker. Have a go at playing the descending bass figure along with the CD.

**Here is the DESCENDING BASS FIGURE
that starts the song:**

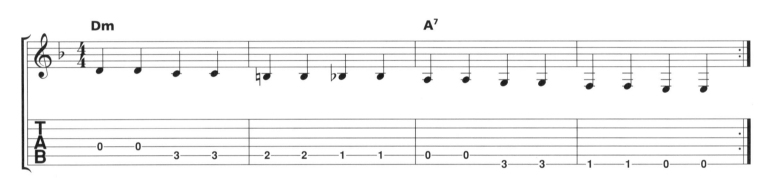

2 BAR CLICK + 8 BAR INTRO

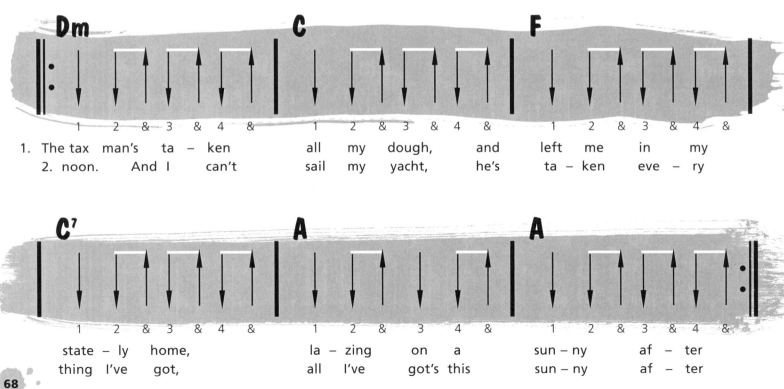

1. The tax man's ta – ken   all   my   dough,   and   left   me   in   my
2. noon.   And I   can't   sail my   yacht,   he's ta – ken   eve – ry

state – ly   home,   la – zing   on a   sun – ny   af – ter
thing I've   got,   all   I've   got's this   sun – ny   af – ter

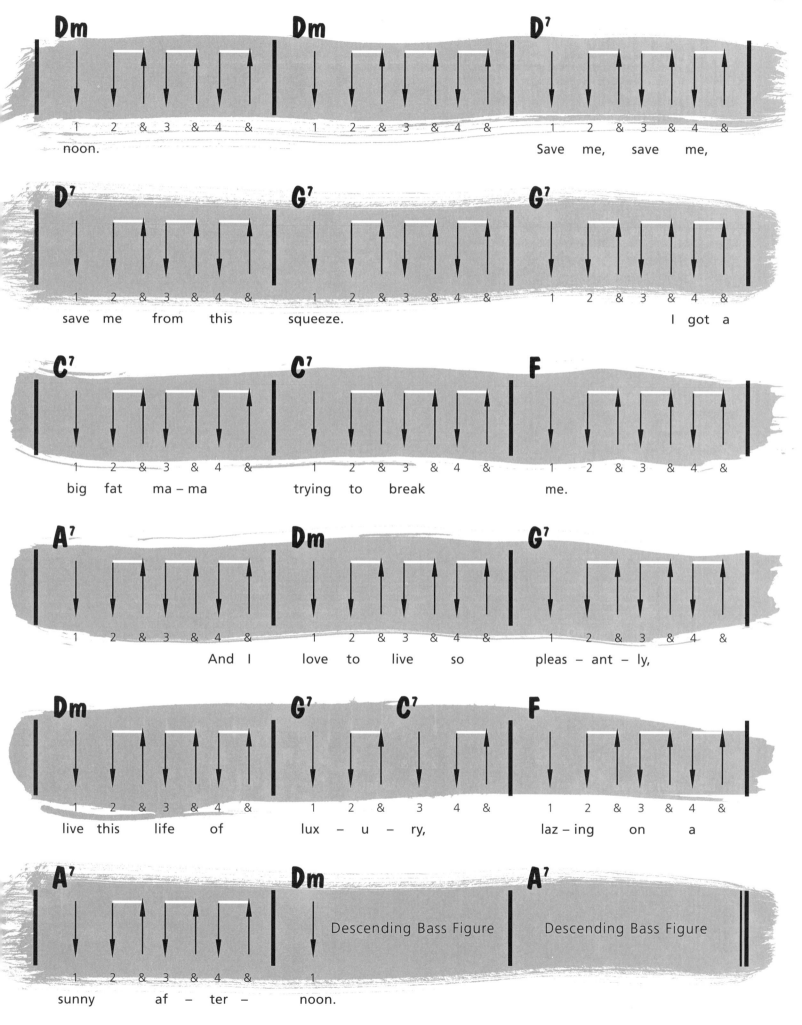

TAINTED LOVE
Words & Music by Ed Cobb

This well-known song was first recorded by Soft Cell, and reached No. 8 in 1982. Many artists and bands such as Shades Apart and Marilyn Manson have subsequently covered it.

This famous chord progression is strummed with mostly downstrokes, but watch out for the anticipation in the second measure. For a heavier rock feel, try the basic two-measure pattern using "power chords" instead of full chords. Power chords are usually just the bottom two or three notes of a barre chord, and add a low crunch to your sound. Check out the TAB below and use all downstrokes for added punch.

Since this tune has been covered so many times in so many different keys, you might need a capo to play along with your favorite version. This one's in **Em;** other popular keys are **F#m** (capo 2nd fret), **Gm** (capo 3rd fret), and **Am** (capo 5th fret).

POWER CHORD RIFF

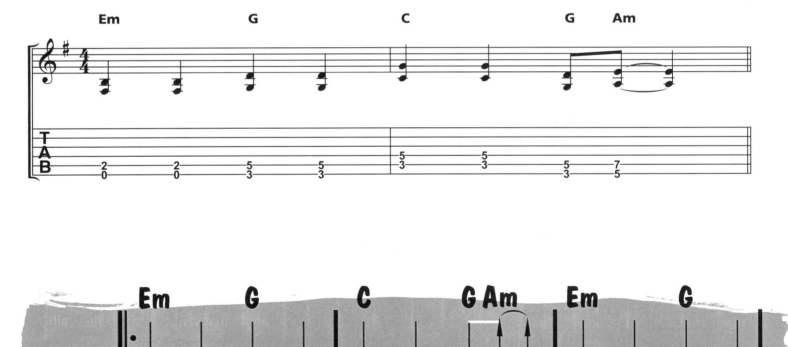

1. Some - times   I feel I've   got to run   a - way,
    we share   seems to go   no - where,

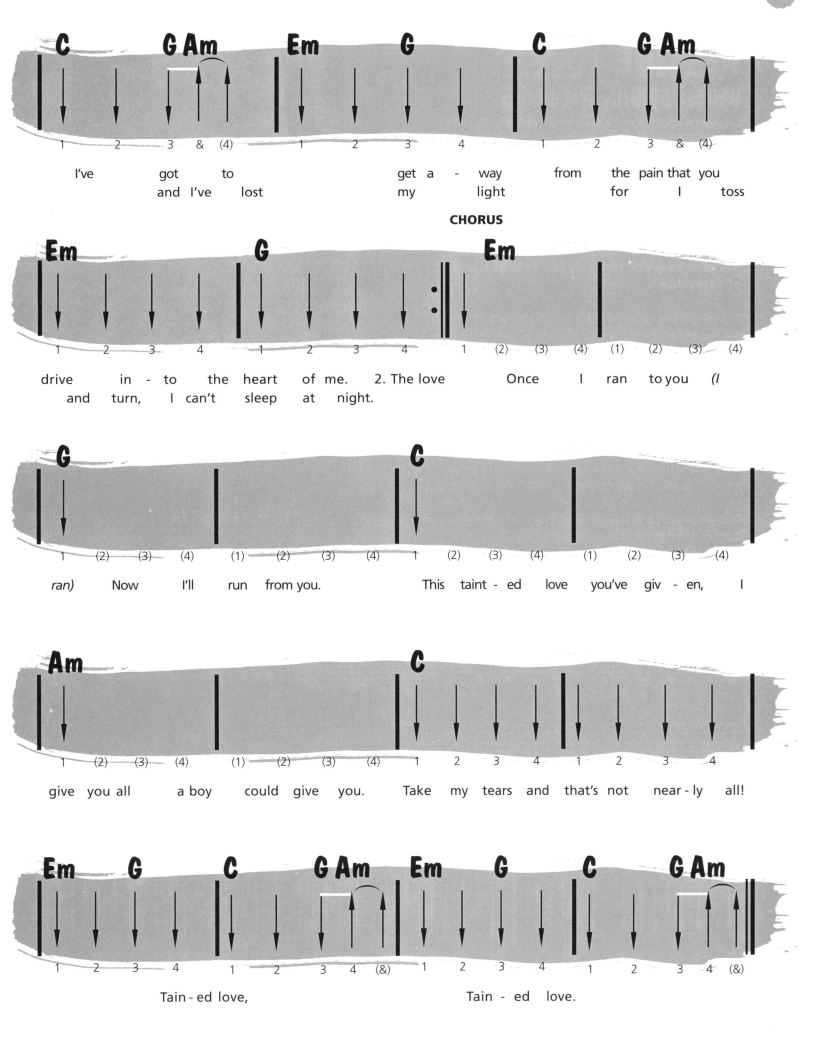

HEY JOE
Written by Billy Roberts

The entire song here is based on a single four-bar chord progression using C, G, D, A, E and E7. Watch out for the tie sign (⌒), used to tie two notes of the same pitch together so that only the first of the tied notes is played. You can see this in bar 3 of "Hey Joe."

To play this bar strum all the marks as shown but leave out the one that falls directly over the 4, letting the previous strum (a chord change to **E7**) ring instead.

You can also try your hand at this catchy chromatic riff which fits perfectly under the chords and is instantly recognizable as the famous bass riff from the Jimi Hendrix smash hit recording of this song.

A chromatic phrase is one which uses notes that are not properly in key. Chromatic phrases usually feature lots of half-step movement in either direction. The timing is easy because the riff is in straight 8ths. Practice it very slowly and evenly before attempting to play it at the correct tempo.

Jimi Hendrix

Here is the main guitar riff:

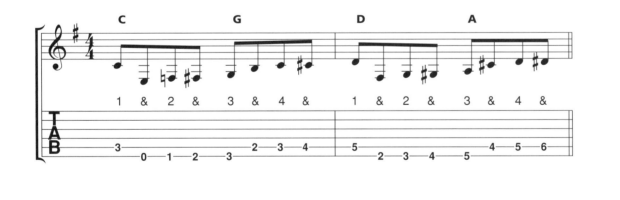

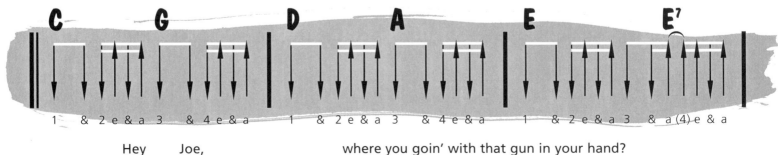

Hey   Joe,   where you goin' with that gun in your hand?

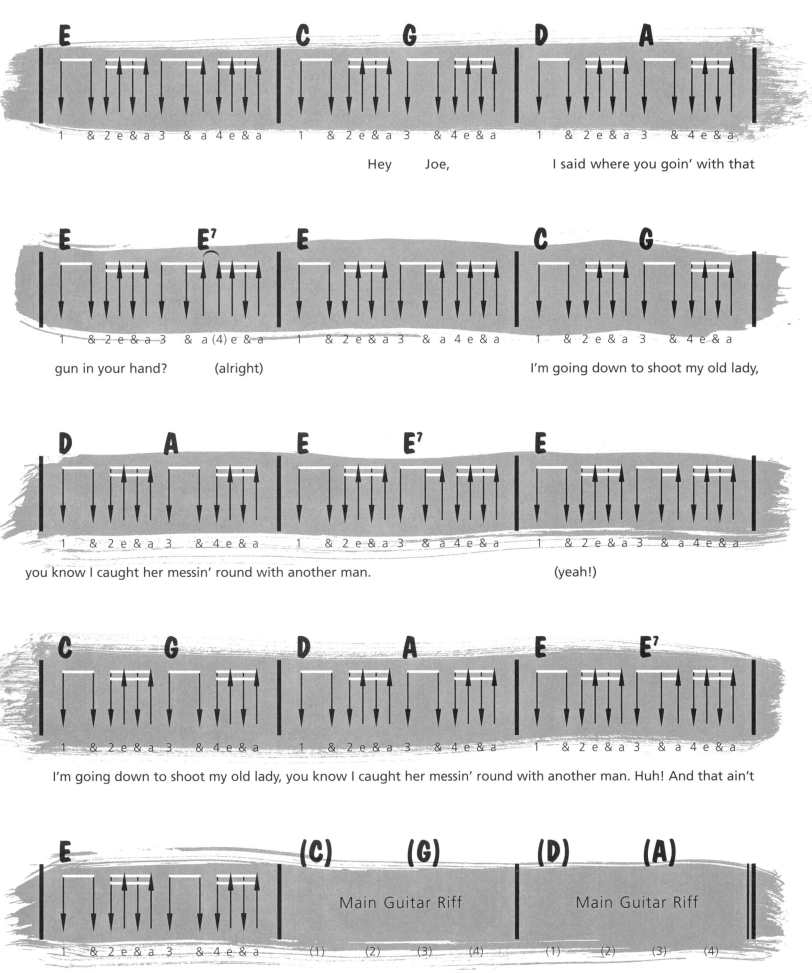

Hey   Joe,   I said where you goin' with that

gun in your hand?   (alright)   I'm going down to shoot my old lady,

you know I caught her messin' round with another man.   (yeah!)

I'm going down to shoot my old lady, you know I caught her messin' round with another man. Huh! And that ain't

too cool.

Bob Dylan

LIKE A ROLLING STONE
Words & Music by Bob Dylan

Dsus2 Chord

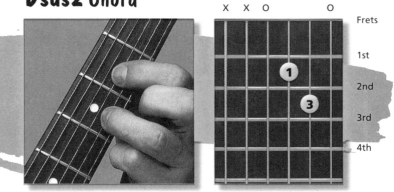

Folk legend Bob Dylan wrote and recorded this song, which reached No. 2 in the charts in 1965. It is featured on the album *Highway 61 Revisited*.

This classic has a basic strumming pattern of 1 2 & 3 4 &, but feel free to squeeze in some extra strums if you can. At a moderate tempo, you should be able to strum 1 2 &-a 3 4 &-a comfortably.

We have another suspended chord in this tune, the **Dsus2** chord, where the third is replaced by the second note in the scale. Use this chord for a little variety over the D major chord during the chorus.

Place your capo at the 3rd fret to play this song along with the original recording.

CAPO 3RD FRET
VERSE

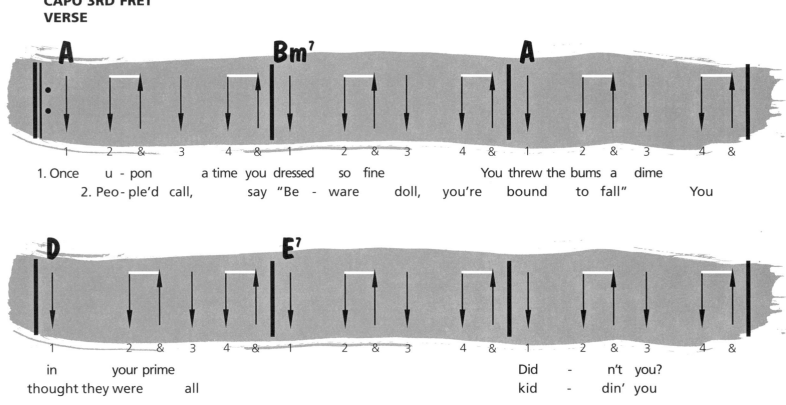

1. Once u-pon a time you dressed so fine You threw the bums a dime
2. Peo-ple'd call, say "Be-ware doll, you're bound to fall" You

in your prime Did - n't you?
thought they were all kid - din' you

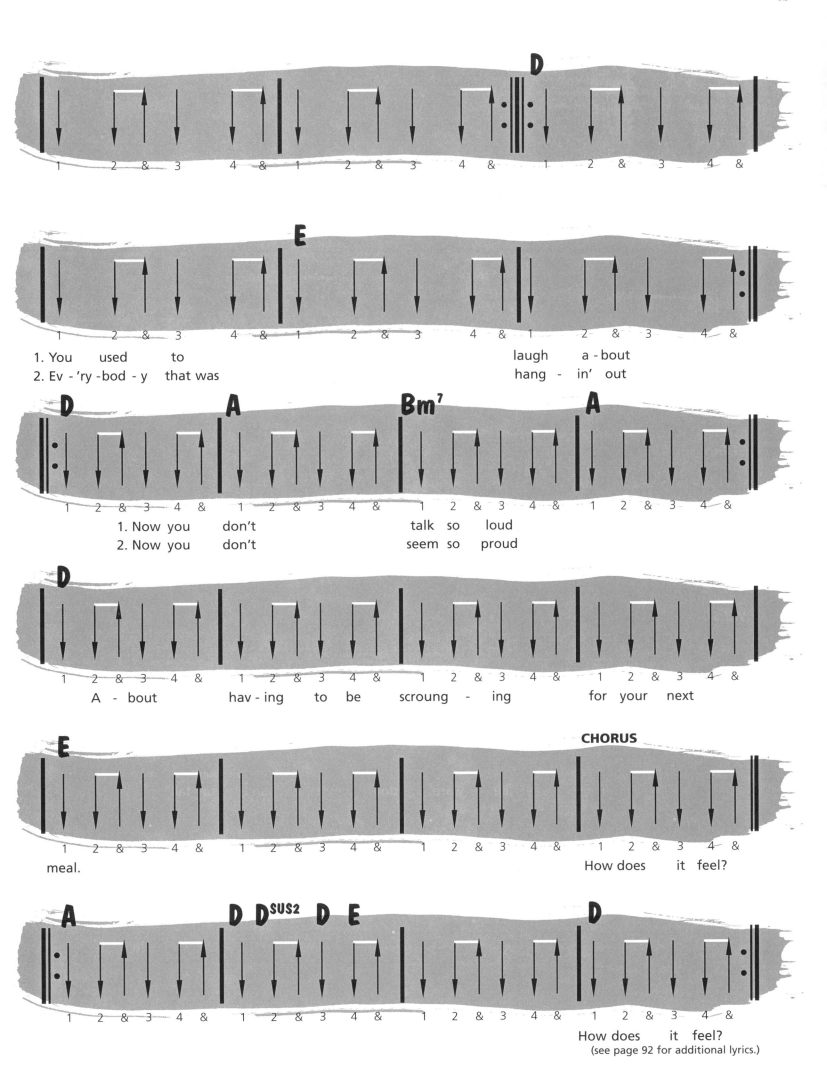

1. You used to   laugh a - bout
2. Ev - 'ry -bod - y that was   hang - in' out

1. Now you don't   talk so loud
2. Now you don't   seem so proud

A - bout   hav - ing to be scroung - ing   for your next

CHORUS

meal.   How does   it feel?

How does   it feel?
(see page 92 for additional lyrics.)

NIGHTS IN WHITE SATIN
Words & Music by Justin Hayward

Taken from their concept album *Days Of Future Passed*, this romantic ballad charted for The Moody Blues on no less than three occasions, in 1967, 1972, and 1979, and uses a new time-signature: 6/8.

This basically means that there are six 8th notes in each bar, as opposed to the four quarter notes you are used to. 6/8 has a kind of lilting rhythm and is commonly used for ballads.

If you're wondering what the difference is between 6/8 and 3/4 (as they both basically add up to the same number of beats), it is simply that you can "feel" **two** main beats in each bar of 6/8 (each beat made up of three 8th notes), whereas in 3/4 it is definitely **three** main beats (each beat made up of two 8th notes). It is a subtle difference but see if you can spot it.

For more on time signatures, see page 84.

When you have mastered the chord changes and strumming pattern for this song, why not try learning the flute solo as well? We've arranged it for guitar, below:

The Moody Blues

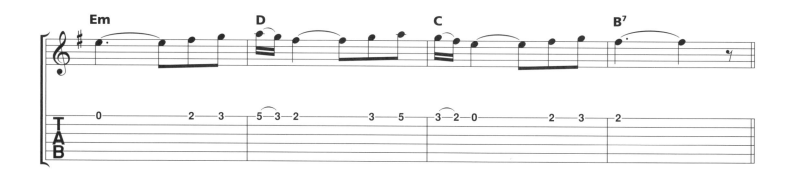

CAPO 3RD FRET

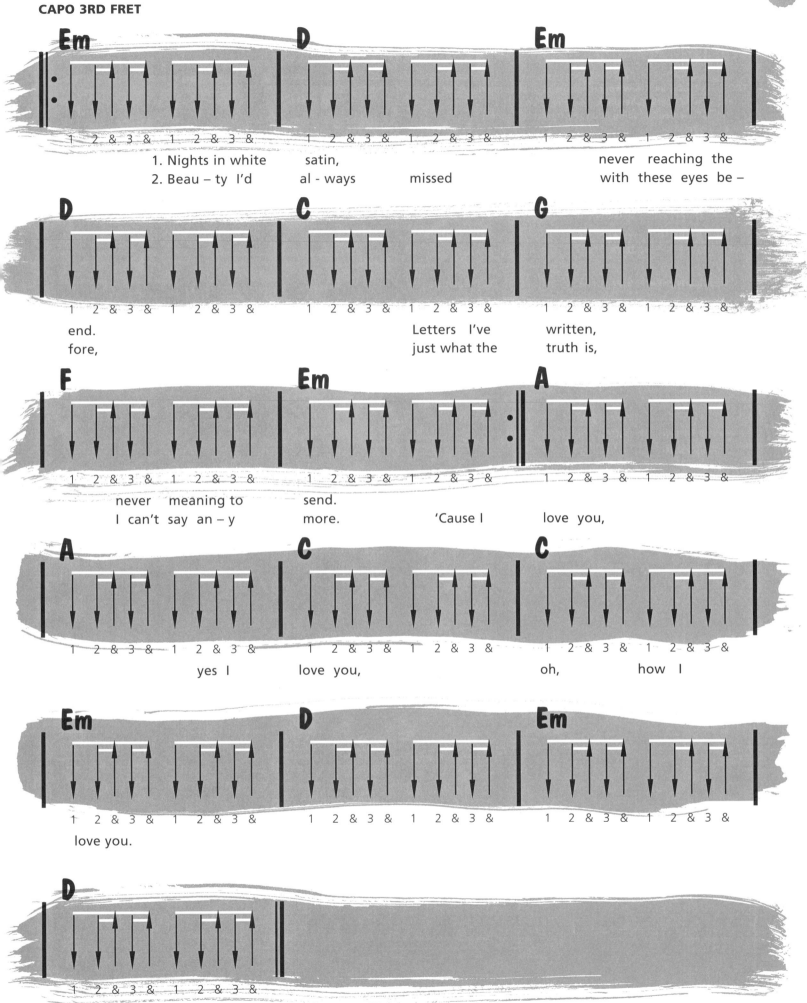

1. Nights in white   satin,   never reaching the
2. Beau – ty I'd   al - ways   missed   with these eyes be –

end.
fore,

Letters I've   written,
just what the   truth is,

never   meaning to   send.   'Cause I   love you,
I can't say an – y   more.

yes I   love you,   oh,   how I

love you.

WHILE MY GUITAR GENTLY WEEPS
Words & Music by George Harrison

Am/G Chord

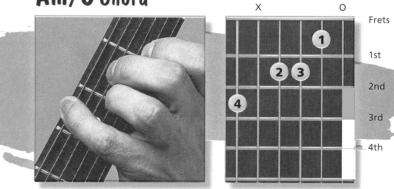

F#m Chord

George Harrison's ballad appeared on The Beatles' *White Album*. It introduces one new chord: Am/G.

We could use an **Am7** for this (try it for contrast) but **Am/G** is preferable because it preserves the descending bass line under the chords. The next chord, **D/F#**, has that bass line moving down one more half step. The **F#m** in the bridge is an **Fm** shape moved up one fret.

The strumming is straight 8ths in the verse, but watch out for the tied chords at the end of the bridge.

This bridge also happens to be in a different key. The song starts in **A minor** but changes into **A major**. This is why the mood seems to change at that point.

George Harrison

2 BAR CLICK + 8 BAR INTRO
VERSE

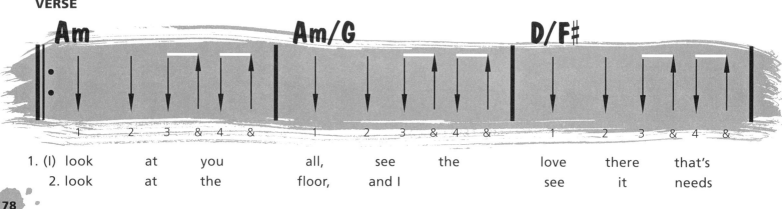

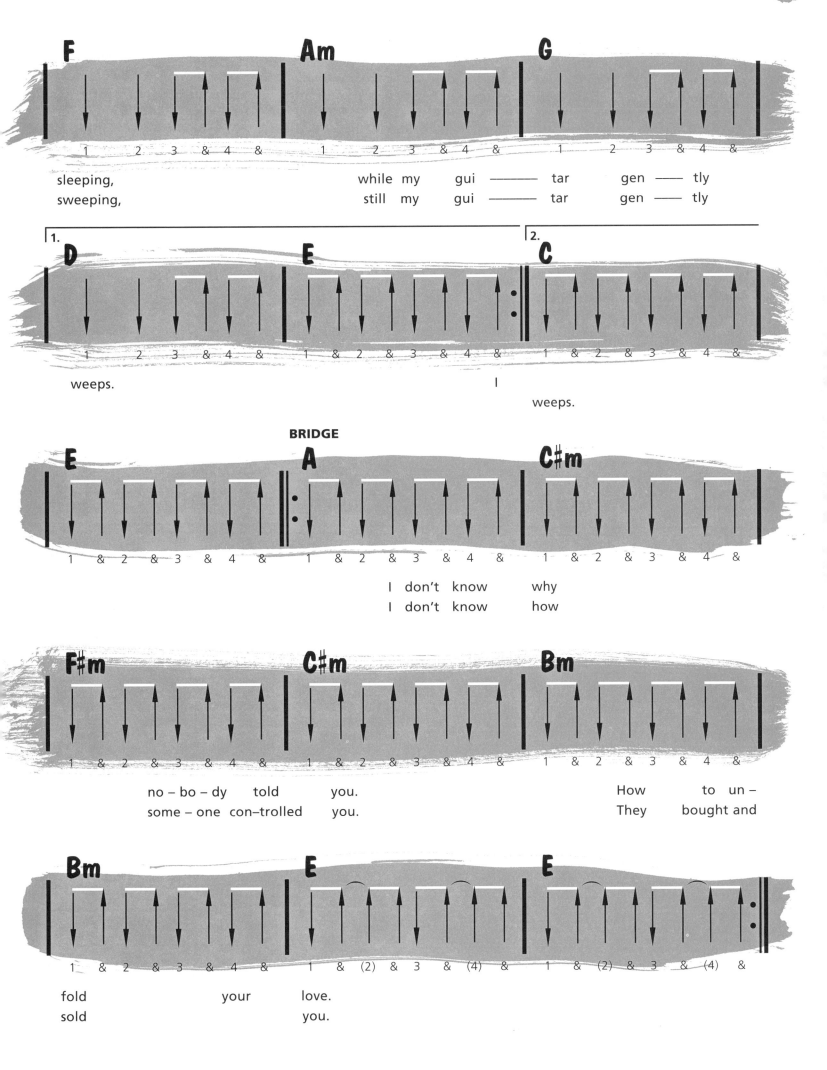

PINBALL WIZARD

Words & Music by
Pete Townshend

This hit by The Who comes from their rock opera *Tommy*.

You are already familiar with **sus4** chords, but for this song, we're going to have to take it up a few frets, to the 7th. Look at the chord on the right—**Bsus4/B***. Start with a partial barre at the 7th fret, using your first finger. To get the bass note, you'll need to use your thumb too— a tricky technique that might need some practice. You also need to mute the 5th string with the side of your thumb. Then place your other fingers down. Now, strum fast while adding and removing your little finger at the 9th fret—and you've got the intro to "Pinball Wizard"!

The strum is also challenging, as it's so fast and also accented in an unusual way. Listen to the CD first, then take a look at the music. See if you can "feel" where the accents should fall. Alternatively, try counting this rhythm accenting the **1** and not counting the (&):

1 2 3 **1** 2 3 **1** 2 3 **1** 2 3 **1** (&) **2** (&)

Now you've almost got it, but there's also the famous intro to learn. We've written it out in TAB, below. Use down strokes to keep the 8th-note **F♯** going, playing the chord only once, on the first beat of the bar.

Bsus4 / B* Chord

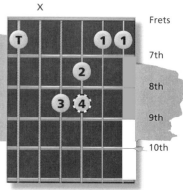

Dsus4 Chord

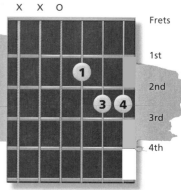

B major Chord

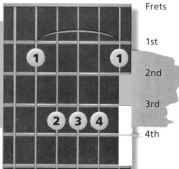

2 BAR CLICK INTRO

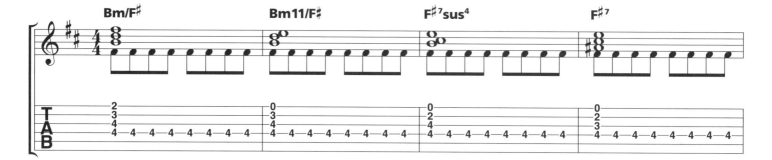

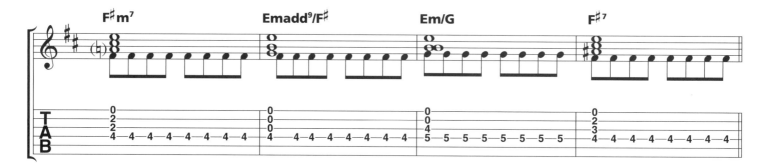

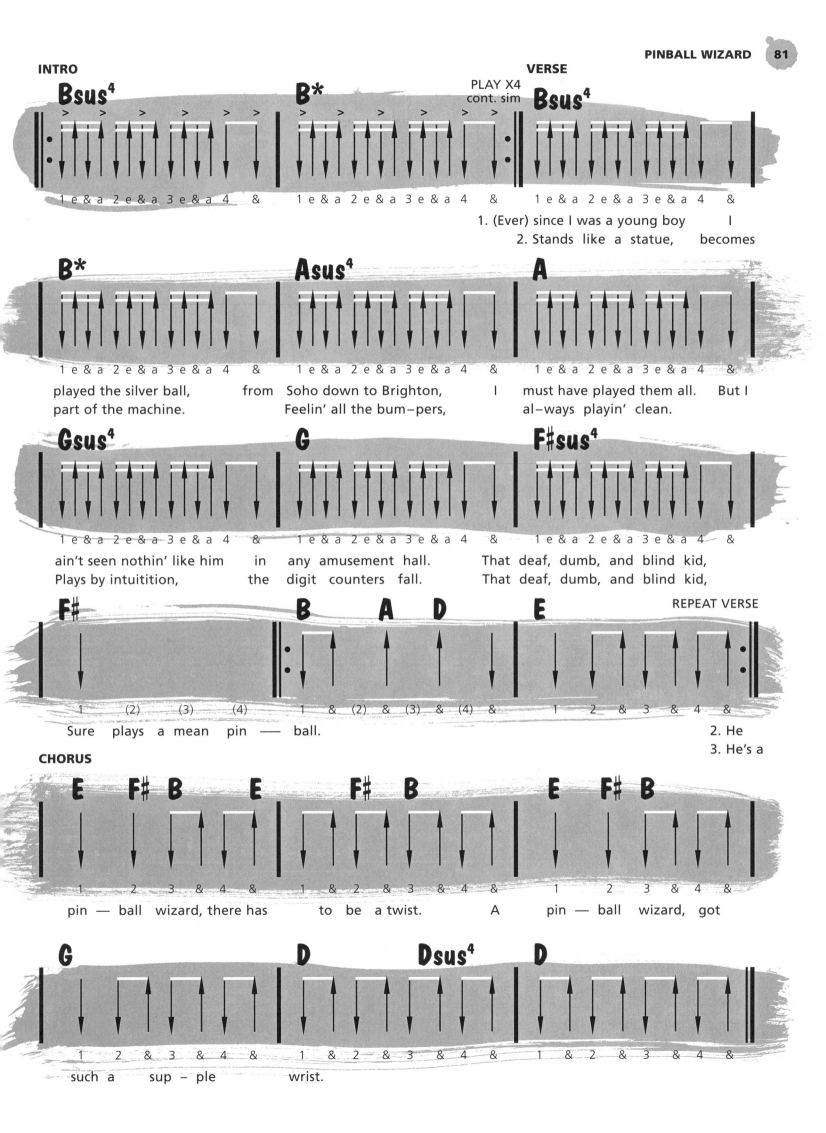

BACK IN BLACK
By Angus Young, Malcolm Young & Brian Johnson

This song from the famous *Back In Black* album hit the charts in 1980.

This rock guitar classic has a great riff over the verse, which is written out below in TAB for you to try. The tempo is slow and steady, so the quick strums shouldn't cause too much trouble. Aim more for the lower strings when strumming this one (like power chords) for a heavier rock sound.

The verse riff has two important but easy lead guitar licks. **Lick 1** is all down in first position, and uses your third and second fingers and some open strings. **Lick 2** calls for you to shift your hand up to the 4th position to grab all the notes on the bottom string.

The strumming pattern in the chorus is mostly downstrokes, but be sure to count out all the rhythms correctly. Take it slowly at first, and keep counting 1-e-&-a 2-e-&-a etc. to get the anticipations right. Although the timing may look tricky at first, it is actually a natural hard-rocking groove that almost plays itself.

AC/DC

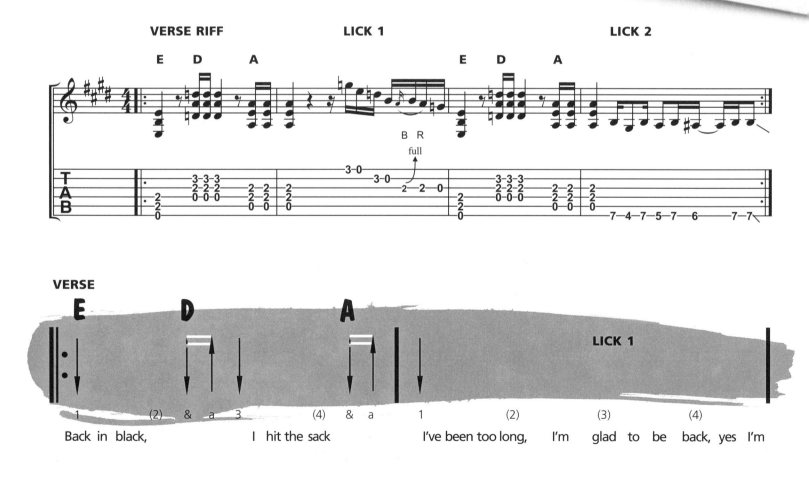

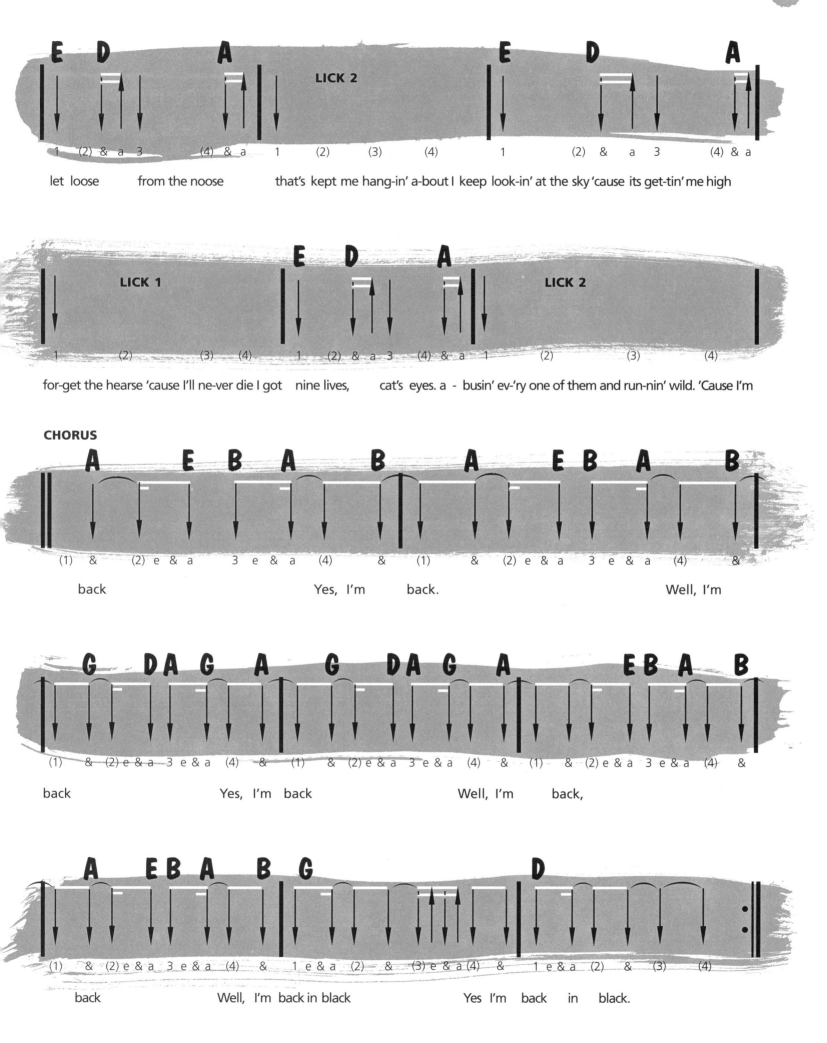

READING MUSIC MADE EASY

THE STAFF

The music we play is written on five equally spaced lines called a **staff**.

The staff is divided into **bars** (or measures) by the use of a vertical line.

Each bar has a fixed number of **beats** in it. A beat is the natural tapping rhythm of a song. Most songs have four beats in each bar, and we can tap our feet or count along with these songs.

1 2 3 4 | 1 2 3 4 | 1 2 3 4

Occasionally, there are three beats in each bar, and we count like this:

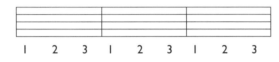

1   2   3 | 1   2   3 | 1   2   3

TIME SIGNATURES

At the beginning of every piece of music there are two numbers, written one above the other. This is called a **time signature**. The top number tells us how many beats are in a bar. The lower number tells us the value of these beats as expressed in the musical notation (this will be explained shortly).

The two most common time signatures in popular music are these:

4/4 is often shown as C, or **common time**.

Once given, the time signature is not repeated, unless the beat changes within a song. This happens only rarely in popular music.

CLEFS

The other symbol we find at the beginning of each staff is called the **treble clef**.

This fixes the pitch of the notes on the staff. The line that passes through the center of the spiral, second up from the bottom, fixes the note G. We will look more at notes and pitch in a moment.

FORM NOTATION (REPEAT SIGNS)

In music there are various standard markings which can be used to abbreviate the layout. When we come to this sign:

it tells us to go back to where this sign appears:

(or sometimes when this does not appear, we return to the beginning) and **repeat** the section.

1ST & 2ND TIME BARS

Sometimes we repeat the whole section, but the ending of the "second time through" can be different from the first time. Thus we have what are called **1st** and **2nd** time bars (or 3rd and 4th for that matter). Here is an example:

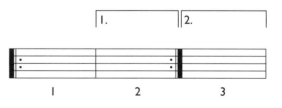

1   2   3

The first time through we play bars 1 and 2. The second time we play bars 1 and 3.

D.C. & D.S.

We often see the letters D.C. and D.S. at the end of a staff line. **D.C.** (from the Italian *da capo*) tells us to return to the beginning ("top"). **D.S.** (*dal segno*) means return to the sign (![segno]). After these letters we see the words **al coda** (**to the coda**) or **al fine** (**to the finish**). The **coda** is the end section of a song, usually short. Here is an example:

Here we play bars 1-3. We are then directed back to bar 2, and continue to bar 3, when the sign (⊕) above the bar line tells us to jump to the coda at bar 4.

Here is another example:

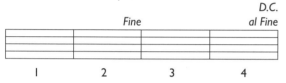

Play bars 1-4. Then return to bar 1, and continue to bar 2, where the word **Fine** (or **end**) tells us to stop. Sometimes coupled with the word **Fine** we see the sign (⌒) over a chord or note. This means you pause on the beat marked, letting the final chord ring. This is a very common ending.

(⁒) means that you should repeat the preceding bar.

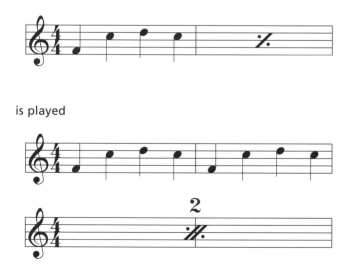

is played

means that you should repeat the preceding two bars.

NOTE VALUES

Now we come to notes and their time values. The notes tell the player exactly what to play, how to play it, and when to play it.

Whole Note:

Half Note:

Quarter Note:

Eighth Note:

Sixteenth Note:

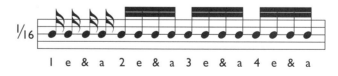

The notes in each diagram all add up to four beats, the beat being one quarter note. Eighth notes and sixteenth notes are joined together with "beams" to make the music easier to read.

So in a piece of music in 4/4 time we count four beats to the bar, each beat being one quarter note:

COUNTING

Many guitar accompaniments consist of strumming eight 8th-notes to each bar of 4/4 time. We still count four quarter-notes, but to maintain an easy rhythm we count 1 & 2 & 3 & 4 &, each syllable being one 8th-note:

A bar in 2/4 time will contain two quarter-note beats per bar:

We can break this counting down further, so with 16th-note rhythms the count would be: 1e&a 2e&a 3e&a 4e&a, each syllable being one 16th-note:

The same principle applies to 3/4 time:

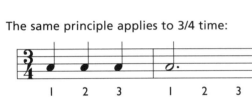

Sometimes we see dotted 8th notes and 16th notes joined together. Again we count four, but the rhythm does not flow smoothly as with eight 8th-notes to the bar, and we count like this:

DOTTED NOTES

Above, we see a half note with a **dot** after it. The dot increases the time value of any note after which it is placed by half.

So, a **dotted half note**: 2 beats + 1 beat = 3 beats.

A **dotted quarter note**: 1 + ½ = 1½ beats.

RESTS

Just as notes tell us when to play, we have **rests** which tell us when not to play. There is a rest which corresponds in value to each type of note.

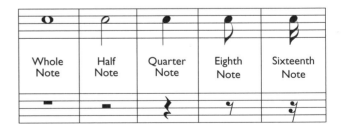

Similarly, dotted rests have the same time values as dotted notes.

A whole bar's rest is generally shown by a whole-note rest, whether or not the music is in 4/4 time.

PITCH

Here is the scale of **C major**.

A **whole step** (W) is made up of **2 half steps** (H), and half steps correspond to the **frets** on your guitar, i.e., **C** to **D** is a whole step or two frets, and **E** to **F** is a half step or one fret.

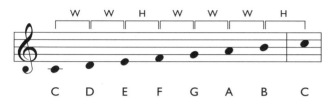

This is an octave and can be repeated up or down the staff.

LEGER LINES

The first C is below the staff and we see that a **leger** line runs through the note. This is an extension of the staff to accommodate the note. Here are more examples:

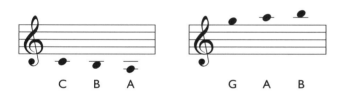

KEY SIGNATURE

At the beginning of each staff line we see, after the treble clef, the **key signature** of the music. This consists of **sharps** or **flats** or, in the case of C major or A minor none at all, and indicates that all notes against which they are set should be raised or lowered by a **half step**.

Here, all **F**s are to be raised by a half step in all octaves.

Here, all **B**s and **E**s are to be lowered by a half step in all octaves:

ACCIDENTALS

It is necessary sometimes to insert sharps or flats that do not occur in the key signature. They are called **accidentals**. In this case we put the sign before the individual note, and its effect lasts for one bar only. The **natural** sign (♮) is also used to countermand a sharp or flat given in the key signature. Again, its effect is for one bar only:

TIES

Finally we come to the curved line called a **tie**, which, in its various functions, will occur in this book.

It has the effect of joining together two notes. When you see two notes of the same pitch tied together you simply play the first one and let it ring on through the note to which it is tied.

These are the basic outlines of reading and understanding written music.

ADDITIONAL LYRICS

BLUE SUEDE SHOES

Verse 1
Well it's one for the money
Two for the show
Three to get ready, now go, cat, go...
But don't you step on my blue
suede shoes.
You can do anything but stay off
of my blue suede shoes.

Verse 2
Well you can knock me down
Step on my face
Slander my name all over the place
Do anything that you want to do
But ah-ah honey lay off of them
shoes...
And don't you step on my blue
suede shoes.
You can do anything but stay off
of my blue suede shoes.

Let's go cats!

Verse 3
You can burn my house, steal my car
Drink my liquor from an old fruit jar
Well do anything that you want to do
But ah-ah honey lay off of my shoes...
And don't you step on my blue
suede shoes.
You can do anything but stay off of
my blue suede shoes.

Verse 4
Well it's one for the money
Two for the show
Three to get ready, now go, go, go...
But don't you step on my blue
suede shoes.
You can do anything but stay off
of my blue suede shoes.

Coda
Well it's blue, blue, blue suede shoes
Blue, blue, blue suede shoes, yeah!
Blue, blue, blue suede shoes, baby!
Blue, blue, blue suede shoes
Well you can do anything but stay off
of my blue suede shoes.

DRIFTWOOD

Verse 1
Everything is open
Nothing is set in stone
Rivers turn to oceans
Oceans tide you home
Home is where the heart is
But your heart had to roam
Drifting over bridges
Never to return
Watching bridges burn.

Chorus
You're driftwood floating underwater
Breaking into pieces, pieces, pieces.
Just driftwood, hollow and of no use
Waterfalls will find you, bind you
Grind you.

Verse 2
Nobody is an island
Everyone has to go
Pillars turn to butter
Butter flying low
Low is where your heart is
But your heart has to grow
Drifting under bridges
Never with the flow.

Bridge
And you really didn't think it would
happen
But it really is the end of the line.

Chorus
So I'm sorry that you've turned
to driftwood
But you've been drifting for a long,
long time.

Verse 3
Everywhere there's trouble
Nowhere's safe to go
Pushes turn to shovels
Shovelling the snow
Frozen you have chosen
The path you wish to go
Drifting now forever
And forever more
Until you reach your shore.

Chorus
You're driftwood floating underwater
Breaking into pieces, pieces, pieces.
Just driftwood, hollow and of no use
Waterfalls will find you, bind you
Grind you, and you...

Bridge
Really didn't think it would happen
But it really is the end of the line.

Chorus
So I'm sorry that you've turned
to driftwood
But you've been drifting for a long,
long time
You've been drifting for a long, long
time
You've been drifting for a long, long
Drifting for a long, long time.

SAIL AWAY

Chorus

Sail away with me honey
I put my heart in your hands
Sail away with me honey now
Now, now.
Sail away with me
What will be will be
I wanna hold you now, now, now.

Verse 2

Crazy skies all wild above me now
Winter howling at my face
And everything I held so dear
Disappeared without a trace
Oh all the times I've tasted love
Never knew quite what I had
Little darling if you hear me now
Never needed you so bad
Spinning round inside my head.

Chorus

Verse 2

I've been talking drunken gibberish
Falling in and out of bars
Trying to get some explanation here
For the way some people are.
How did it ever come so far?

Repeat Chorus x 2

Verse 3

Sail away with me honey
I put my heart in your hands
You'll break me up if you put me
down, whoa———.
Sail away with me
What will be will be
I wanna hold you now, now, now.

WILD WOOD

Verse 1

High tide, mid-afternoon
People fly by in the traffic's boom
Knowing just where you're blowing
Getting to where
You should be going.

Verse 2

Don't let them get you down
Making you feel guilty about
Golden rain will bring you riches
All the good things you deserve now.

Verse 3

Climbing, forever trying
Find your way out
Of the wild, wild wood.
Now there's no justice
You've only yourself
That you can trust in.

Verse 4

And I said, high tide, mid-afternoon
People fly by in the traffic's boom
Knowing just where you're blowing
Getting to where
You should be going.

Verse 5

Day by day, your world fades away
Waiting to feel all the dreams that say
Golden rain will bring you riches
All the good things you deserve now
And I say...

Verse 6

Climbing, forever trying
You're gonna find your way out
Of the wild, wild wood.
I said, you're gonna find your way out
Of the wild, wild wood.

ROLL WITH IT

Verse 1

You gotta roll with it
You gotta take your time
You gotta say what you say
Don't let anybody get in your way
'Cause it's all too much for me to take.

Verse 2

Don't ever stand aside
Don't ever be denied
You wanna be who you'd be
If you're coming with me.
I think I've got a feeling I've lost
inside
I think I'm gonna take me away
and hide
I'm thinking things that I just can't
abide.

Bridge

I know the roads down which your
life will drive
I find the key that lets you slip inside
Kiss the girl, she's not behind the door
But you know I think I recognize
your face
But I've never seen you before.

Repeat Verse 1

Instrumental

Repeat Bridge

Repeat Verse 1

Coda

Don't ever stand aside
Don't ever be denied
You wanna be who you'd be
If you're coming with me.

I think I've got a feeling I've lost
inside. *(repeat ad lib to fade)*

20TH CENTURY BOY

Verse 1
Friends say it's fine
Friends say it's good
Everybody says it's
Just like Robin Hood.
I move like a cat
Charge like a ram
Sting like a bee, babe!
I wanna be your man.

Chorus
But it's plain to see
You were meant for me, yeah
I'm your boy
Your Twentieth Century toy.

Verse 2
Friends say it's fine
Friends say it's good
Everybody says it's
Just like Robin Hood.
Fly like a plane, drive like a car
Bark like a hound, babe!
I wanna be your man.

Chorus 2
But it's plain to see
You were meant for me, yeah
I'm your toy
Your Twentieth Century boy.

Bridge
Twentieth century toy
I wanna be your boy.
Twentieth century boy
I wanna be your toy.
Twentieth century toy
I wanna be your boy.
Twentieth century boy
I wanna be your toy.

Repeat Verse 1

Repeat Chorus

Repeat Bridge

SHE LOVES YOU

Intro
She loves you, yeah, yeah, yeah
She loves you, yeah, yeah, yeah
She loves you, yeah, yeah, yeah, yeah.

Verse 1
You think you've lost your love
Well I saw her yesterday
It's you she's thinking of
And she told me what to say
She says she loves you
And you know that can't be bad
Yes, she loves you
And you know you should be glad.

Verse 2
She said you hurt her so
She almost lost her mind
But now she says she knows
You're not the hurting kind
She says she loves you
And you know that can't be bad
Yes, she loves you
And you know you should be glad.

Chorus
She loves you, yeah, yeah, yeah
She loves you, yeah, yeah, yeah
With a love like that
You know you should be glad.

Verse 3
You know it's up to you
I think it's only fair
Pride can hurt you too
Apologise to her
Because she loves you
And you know that can't be bad
Yes, she loves you
And you know you should be glad.

Chorus
She loves you, yeah, yeah, yeah
She loves you, yeah, yeah, yeah
With a love like that
You know you should be glad
With a love like that
You know you should be glad
With a love like that
You know you should be glad
Yeah, yeah, yeah
Yeah, yeah, yeah, yeah.

FATHER AND SON

Verse 1
It's not time to make a change
Just relax, take it easy
You're still young, that's your fault
There's so much you have to know
Find a girl, settle down
If you want, you can marry
Look at me; I am old, but I'm happy.

Verse 2
I was once like you are now
And I know that it's not easy
To be calm when you've found
something going on
But take your time, think a lot
Think of everything you've got
For you will still be here tomorrow
But your dreams may not.

Verse 3
How can I try to explain?
When I do, he turns away again
It's always been the same, same old story
From the moment I could talk
I was ordered to listen
Now, there's a way and I know
That I have to go away
I know I have to go.

Verse 4
It's not time to make a change
Just sit down, take it slowly
You're still you, that's your fault
There's so much you have to go through
Find a girl, settle down
If you want, you can marry
Look at me; I am old, but I'm happy.

Verse 5
All the times that I've cried
Keepin' all the things I knew inside
It's hard, but it's harder to ignore it
If they were right, I'd agree
But it's them they know, not me
Now, there's a way and I know
That I have to go away
I know I have to go.

SUNNY AFTERNOON

Verse 1
The tax man's taken all my dough
And left me in my stately home
Lazing on a sunny afternoon
And I can't sail my yacht
He's taken everything I've got
All I've got's this sunny afternoon.

Chorus
Save me, save me, save me from
this squeeze
I got a big fat mama trying to
break me.
And I love to live so pleasantly
Live this life of luxury
Lazing on a sunny afternoon.
In the summertime
In the summertime
In the summertime.

Verse 2
My girlfriend's run off with my car
And gone back to her ma and pa
Telling tales of drunkenness and
cruelty.
Now I'm sitting here
Sipping at my ice cold beer
Lazing on a sunny afternoon.

Chorus 2
Help me, help me, help me sail away
Well give me two good reasons
Why I oughta stay.
'Cause I love to live so pleasantly
Live this life of luxury
Lazing on a sunny afternoon.
In the summertime
In the summertime
In the summertime.

Chorus 3
Save me, save me, save me from
this squeeze
I got a big fat mama trying to
break me.
And I love to live so pleasantly
Live this life of luxury
Lazing on a sunny afternoon.
In the summertime
In the summertime
In the summertime
In the summertime
In the summertime.

TAINTED LOVE

Verse 1
Sometimes I feel
I've got to run away
I've got to get away
From the pain that you drive into the
heart of me
The love we share
Seems to go nowhere
And I've lost my light
For I toss and turn, I can't sleep at
night.

Chorus
Once I ran to you (I ran)
Now I'll run from you
This tainted love you've given
I give you all a boy could give you
Take my tears and that's not nearly all!
Tainted love
Tainted love

Verse 2
Now I know
I've got to run away
I've got to get away
You don't really want it any more from
me
To make things right
You need someone to hold you tight
And you think love is to pray
But I'm sorry I don't pray that way

Chorus

Verse 3
Don't touch me, please
I cannot stand the way you tease
I love you though you hurt me so
Now I'm gonna pack my things and go
Tainted love, tainted love (x 2)
Touch me baby, tainted love (x 2)
Tainted love (x 3)

HEY JOE

Verse 1
Hey Joe, where you goin' with that
gun in your hand?
Hey Joe, I said where you goin' with
that gun in your hand?
I'm going out to shoot my old lady
You know I caught her messin' round
with another man.
I'm going down to shoot my old lady
You know I caught her messin' round
with another man.
(And that ain't too cool.)

Verse 2
Hey Joe, I heard you shot your woman
down, you shot her down now.
Hey Joe, I heard you shot your lady
down, shot her down to the ground.
Yes, I did, I shot her
You know I caught her messin' round,
messin' round town.
I did, I shot her, you know I caught my
old lady messin' around town.
And I gave her the gun, I shot her!

Guitar solo

Verse 3
Hey Joe, where you gonna run to
now?
Hey Joe, where you gonna run to now
(where you gonna go)?
Well, I'm going way down south
Way down to Mexico Way, alright!
Well, I'm going way down south
Way down where I can be free
Ain't no hang man gonna
He ain't gonna put a rope around me.
(You'd better believe, right now.)
Hey Joe, you'd better run now.

LIKE A ROLLING STONE

Verse 1

Once upon a time you dressed so fine
You threw the bums a dime in your prime
Didn't you?
People'd call, say "Beware doll, you're
bound to fall"
You thought they were all kiddin' you
You used to laugh about
Everybody that was hangin' out
Now you don't talk so loud
Now you don't seem so proud
About having to be scrounging for
your next meal

Chorus

How does it feel
How does it feel
To be without a home
Like a complete unknown
Like a rolling stone?

Verse 2

You've gone to the finest school all
right Miss Lonely
But you know you only used to get
juiced in it
And nobody's ever taught you how to
live on the street
And now find out you're gonna have
to get used to it
You said you'd never compromise
With the mystery tramp, but now you
realize
He's not selling any alibis
As you stare into the vacuum of his
eyes
And ask him do you want to make a
deal?

Chorus

Verse 3

You never turned around to see the
frowns on the jugglers and the clowns
When they all come down and did
tricks for you
You never understood that it ain't no
good
You shouldn't let other people get your
kicks for you
You used to ride on the chrome horse
with your diplomat
Who carried on his shoulder a Siamese
cat
Ain't it hard when you discovered that
He really wasn't where it's at
After he took from you everything he
could steal.

Chorus

Verse 4

Princess on the steeple and all the
pretty people
They're drinkin', thinkin' that they got
it made
Exchanging all kinds of precious gifts
and things
But you'd better lift your diamond
ring, you'd better pawn it babe
You used to be so amused
At Napoleon in rags and the language
that he used
Go to him now, he calls you you, can't
refuse
When you got nothing, you got
nothing to lose
You're invisible now, you got no secrets
to conceal

Chorus

NIGHTS IN WHITE SATIN

Verse 1

Nights in white satin
Never reaching the end
Letters I've written
Never meaning to send.
Beauty I'd always missed
With these eyes before
Just what the truth is
I can't say anymore.

Chorus

'Cause I love you
Yes I love you
Oh, how I love you.

Verse 2

Gazing at people
Some hand in hand
Just what I'm doing
They can't understand.
Some try to tell me
Thoughts they cannot defend
Just what you want to be
You'll be in the end.

Chorus

And I love you
Yes I love you
Oh, how I love you.

Repeat Verse 1

Repeat Chorus x 2

WHILE MY GUITAR GENTLY WEEPS

Verse 1
I look at you all, see the love there that's sleeping
While my guitar gently weeps.
I look at the floor and I see it needs sweeping
Still my guitar gently weeps.

Bridge 1
I don't know why nobody told you
How to unfold your love
I don't know how someone controlled you
They bought and sold you.

Verse 2
I look at the world and I notice it's turning
While my guitar gently weeps.
With every mistake we must surely be learning
Still my guitar gently weeps.

Guitar solo

Bridge 2
I don't know how, you were diverted
You were perverted too.
I don't know how you were inverted
No one alerted you.

Verse 3
I look at you all, see the love there that's sleeping
While my guitar gently weeps.
I look at you all...
Still my guitar gently weeps.

PINBALL WIZARD

Verse 1
Ever since I was a young boy
I played the silver ball
From Soho down to Brighton
I must have played 'em all.
But I ain't seen nothin' like him
In any amusement hall
That deaf, dumb, and blind kid
Sure plays a mean pinball.

Verse 1
He stands like a statue
Becomes part of the machine
Feelin' all the bumpers
Always playin' clean.
Plays by intuitition
The digit counters fall
That deaf, dumb, and blind kid
Sure plays a mean pinball.

Chorus
He's a pinball wizard
There has to be a twist
A pinball wizard
Got such a supple wrist.
How do you think he does it?
(I don't know)
What makes him so good?

Verse 3
Ain't got no distractions
Can't hear no buzzes and bells
Don't see no lights a-flashin'
Plays by sense of smell.
Always gets a replay
Never see him fall
That deaf, dumb, and blind kid
Sure plays a mean pinball.

Bridge
I thought I was the body table king
But I just handed my pinball crown to him.

Instrumental

Verse 4
He's been on my fav'rite table
He can beat my best
His disciples lead him in
And he just does the rest.
He's got crazy flippin' fingers
Never see him fall
That deaf, dumb, and blind kid
Sure plays a mean pinball.

BACK IN BLACK

Verse 1
Back in black, I hit the sack
I've been too long, I'm glad to be back, yes I'm
Let loose from the noose
That's kept me hangin' about
I keep lookin' at the sky 'cause its gettin' me high
Forget the hearse 'cause I'll never die
I got nine lives, cat's eyes
Abusin' every one of them and runnin' wild.

Chorus
'Cause I'm back
Yes, I'm back
Well, I'm back
Yes, I'm back
Well, I'm back, back
Well, I'm back in black
Yes I'm back in black.

Verse 2
Back in the back of a Cadillac
Number one with a bullet, I'm a power pack
Yes, I'm in a bang with the gang
They gotta catch me if they want me to hang
'Cause I'm back on the track, and I'm beatin' the flack
Nobody's gonna get me on another rap
So look at me now, I'm just makin' my play
Don't try to push your luck, just get outta my way.

Chorus

Instrumental

Chorus

Instrumental

Chorus

The Complete Rock & Pop Guitar Player
Part 3

INTRODUCTION

Welcome to *The Complete Rock & Pop Guitar Player Part 3*. If you're reading this then you've completed Parts 1 and 2 of the course, and you're well on your way to becoming an accomplished guitarist.

You are now familiar with playing from strumming patterns, chord boxes and lyrics, and have also started to read guitar tablature. **Part 3** will feature more TAB, new chords and more well-known hit songs, as well as a section on guitar effects which explains the many sounds available to an electric guitarist.

The songs are graded as before, introducing new chords, strumming patterns or other techniques as you go along, and full lyrics are included at the back of the book.

ELECTRONIC EFFECTS FOR GUITAR

One of the great things about amplification is that you can alter the sound of your guitar *en route* to the amplifier with the use of electronic sound effects. To do this you will need one extra cable per effect.

If you have more than one effect it is best for your own mobility to have a long cable between the guitar and the first effect, then very short "patch cords" between the effects themselves to keep down the level of unwanted electrical interference. Finally, a long cable between the last effect and the amplifier will give you greater flexibility in positioning yourself for easy access to the pedals.

VOLUME PEDALS

These provide foot-controlled volume level changes. They are very useful as they leave your hands free to concentrate on playing. As this was one of the first "gimmicks" to become available to the electric guitar player it is probably for this reason that effects boxes are known as pedals.

"WAH-WAH" PEDALS

Trumpet players use a mute to get a wah-wah sound; guitarists use a pedal. Wah-wahs have a filter which shifts the emphasis of the sound from bass to treble. With the heel down, the lower frequencies are boosted, and with the toe down, the higher frequencies are boosted.

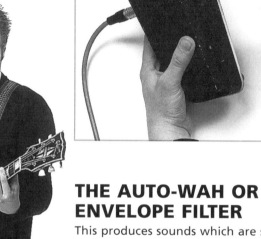

THE AUTO-WAH OR ENVELOPE FILTER

This produces sounds which are similar to a wah-wah pedal. However, rather than having the filter responding to the position of the foot, it responds to the dynamics of your playing. In other words, hitting the strings harder increases treble emphasis and playing lightly produces more bass response.

GRAPHIC EQUALIZER

This device is a sophisticated form of tone control. It allows you to boost or cut many more frequencies than the bass/treble controls on your guitar or amplifier. Using a graphic equalizer opens the door to a completely new spectrum of sounds and for that reason is a very useful effect.

FUZZ AND OVERDRIVE PEDALS AND EFFECTS

Both these types of pedals produce basically the same effect. They overload (overdrive) a section of the circuit of the pedal or the amplifier pre-amp. This gives the notes or chords a much fuller sound and produces much more sustain. The pedals also tend to boost the treble (or top) frequencies of the sound, so it is better to buy one which incorporates a tone control to counteract this. You will find that changing the volume setting on your guitar will alter the intensity of the fuzz.

THE COMPRESSOR

Here is a graph of a guitar string being plucked:

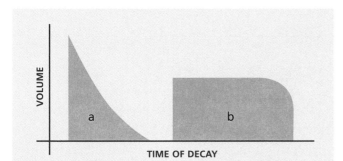

The volume refers to the loudness of the note and the time of decay to the length of time it lasts. Example (a) shows a natural sound and example (b) a compressed one. You will see that the natural sound starts loudly and dies away, whereas the compressed one starts at half the volume but stays there for much longer before quickly dying away. This is what a compressor does. It gives sustain, and is very useful for providing the "pedal steel" type sound which is synonymous with country music.

CHORUS PEDAL

One of the most useful effects for a beginner is the chorus pedal which gives a pleasant jangly sound to your chords. The unit achieves this effect by constantly altering the frequency (in cycles) of a given note (or notes) to just above, and just below, its original pitch.

ECHO UNITS AND REVERB

Along with distortion, reverb is possibly the most useful effect to have in your amplifier. Reverb makes your guitar sound as though it is in a large room or hall. This is great for getting a fuller sound at lower volumes and goes very well with chorus.

Echo units duplicate your notes at a variety of times after the note you have played. Short echoes will thicken your sound; longer echoes can work well on lead solos. The trick is to adjust the time delay, the number of repeats and the volume of the echo compared to the original note, for the best musical effect.

ANALOG DELAY

Analog delay uses a technique generally referred to as the "bucket brigade device" which simply passes the sound through a series of stages (or buckets) until it emerges from the end of the delay line later (in time) than the original sound, which is allowed to pass through the unit unaffected. You can usually mix the volume of the affected and unaffected signal to attain the amount of echo you require.

DIGITAL DELAY

Digital delay is generally accepted as offering the highest fidelity and is therefore more expensive. A typical unit works by sampling the sound and immediately converting it from an audio signal into a digital code, which represents the voltage value. This code word then passes down a series of stages called shift registers and when it emerges it will have been "delayed" before being decoded back into an audio signal at its original voltage level.

The advantage of this technique is that the decoder at the end of the line recognizes only the code word and not the noise which may have accumulated to distort it. So when it changes the code back into audio signal voltage it will sound a great deal closer to the original sound than is possible with other types of units.

MULTI-EFFECTS UNITS

The other type of device you may wish to consider is a multi-effect unit, for example, the Line6 POD. This combines many of the effects previously mentioned into one small compact unit. Using a foot pedal in conjunction allows you to switch easily and quickly between effects, for instance when you're playing solos. It all depends on your budget and the range of effects you're looking for.

MRS. ROBINSON
Words & Music by Paul Simon

Simon & Garfunkel were one of the most popular male duos of the 1960s. "Mrs. Robinson," taken from the film *The Graduate*, charted in 1968 and 1969 with its catchy chorus and acoustic-driven verse.

There are no new chords for this song. For the strumming pattern you need to play the root note of the chord with your thumb, and then strum the chord. Watch out for the ties in bars 5 and 13. Play the upstrum, then count "1" and play on the "&."

Below is the guitar riff that links the chorus to the verse. There are two ways of playing this. You can play the open 6th string with your thumb, and use your fingers to play the higher notes.

Alternatively, you can use a pick to play the 6th-string notes. If you find the timing tricky remember that all the 6th-string Es are on the beat, so fit the higher notes to them rather than the other way round.

Simon & Garfunkel

MAIN GUITAR RIFF

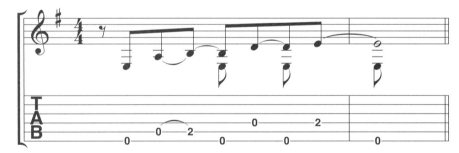

CAPO 3RD FRET
4 BAR "FADE IN" INTRO

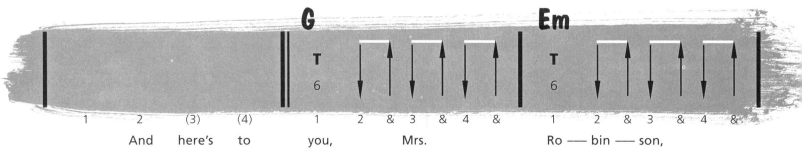

And here's to you, Mrs. Ro — bin — son,

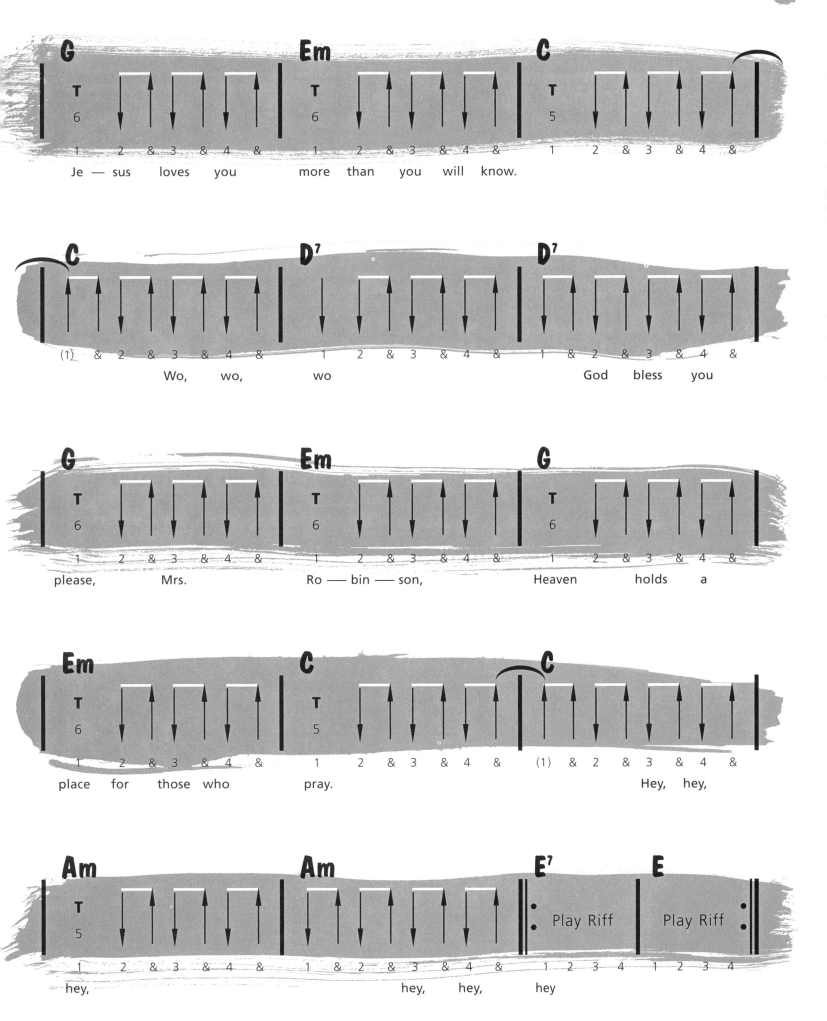

YELLOW

Words & Music by
Guy Berryman, Jon Buckland,
Will Champion & Chris Martin

Bsus4

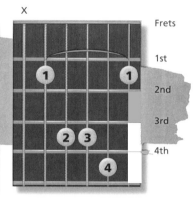

F#6 Chord

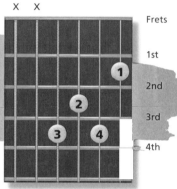

Emaj7

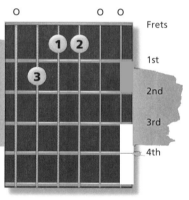

For this recent hit by Coldplay we need to learn three new chords: **Bsus4**, **F#6** and **Emaj7**.

If you find the barre version of **Bsus4** too hard, just use the four-string **B** chord and add the little finger on the 5th fret of the 2nd string. Another way to cheat at this (which happens to fit this song) is to hold the four-string **B** chord and lift your first finger off the top string. Strictly speaking this isn't a **sus4** but it is close enough to suit "**Yellow**."

This **F#6** is an abbreviated version of the full **F#6** chord. Think of it as a half-barre **F** moved to the second fret with the 4th finger adding an extra note. You should find the **Emaj7** easy. This shape is easier to play than some of the more common **Emaj7** shapes and fits the chorus.

The **G#m** on the chorus is simply an **F#m** shape (which you learned in "**While My Guitar Gently Weeps**" in **Part 2**) moved up two frets.

The strumming on "**Yellow**" is steady 8ths throughout.

VERSE

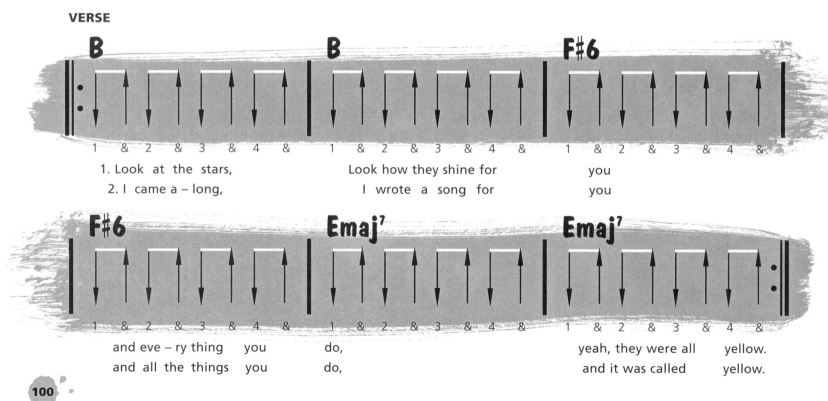

1. Look at the stars,   Look how they shine for   you
2. I came a – long,   I wrote a song for   you

and eve – ry thing   you   do,   yeah, they were all   yellow.
and all the things   you   do,   and it was called   yellow.

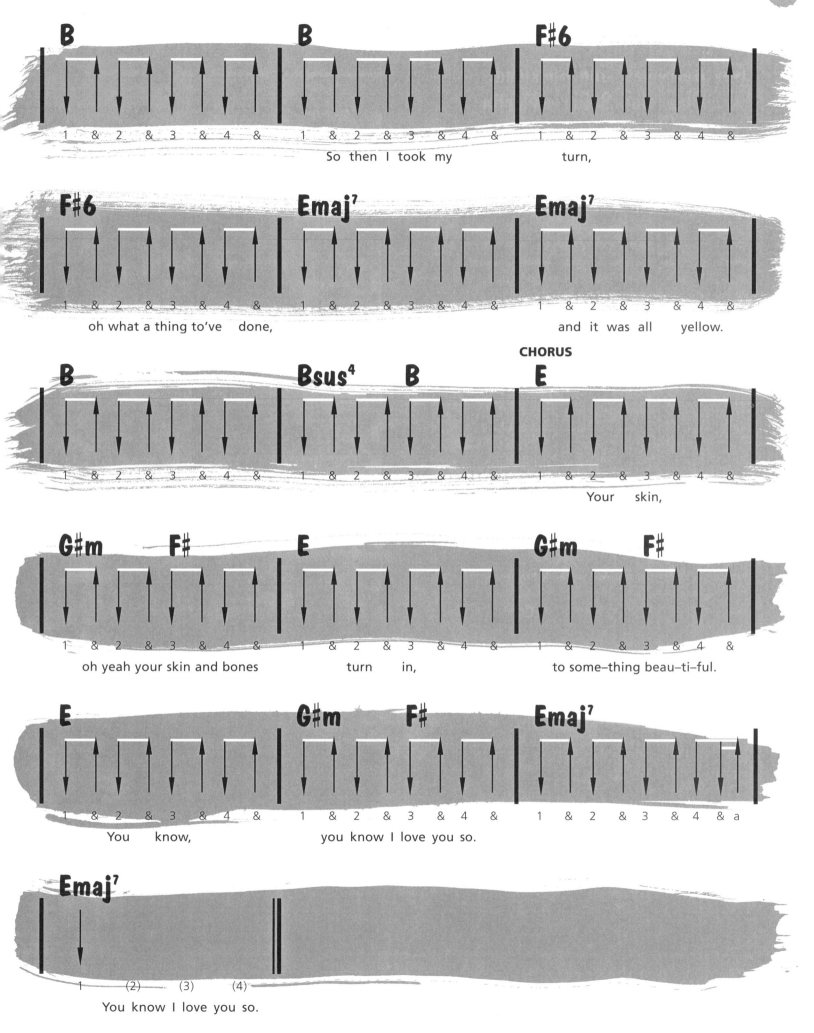

A WHITER SHADE OF PALE
Words & Music by Keith Reid & Gary Brooker

Procol Harum

This beautiful ballad by Procol Harum is a classic 1960s pop song that went to No.3 in the U.S.

This song uses five inversions: **C/B, Am/G, F/E, Dm/C,** and **G/D**. This is because the song's progression is marked by a descending bass line; the inversions help to reproduce it. With the strum pattern you are directed to pick the bass note on its own before you hit the chord.

Dm/C Chord

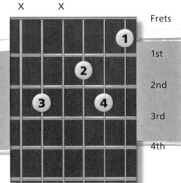

G/D Chord

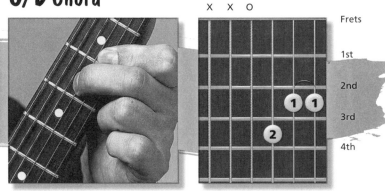

Here's the intro melody. You can either count eight bars from the beginning and then start strumming, or you could try playing this first, and then move on to the strumming.

INTRO

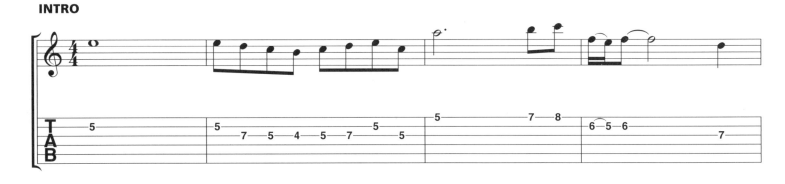

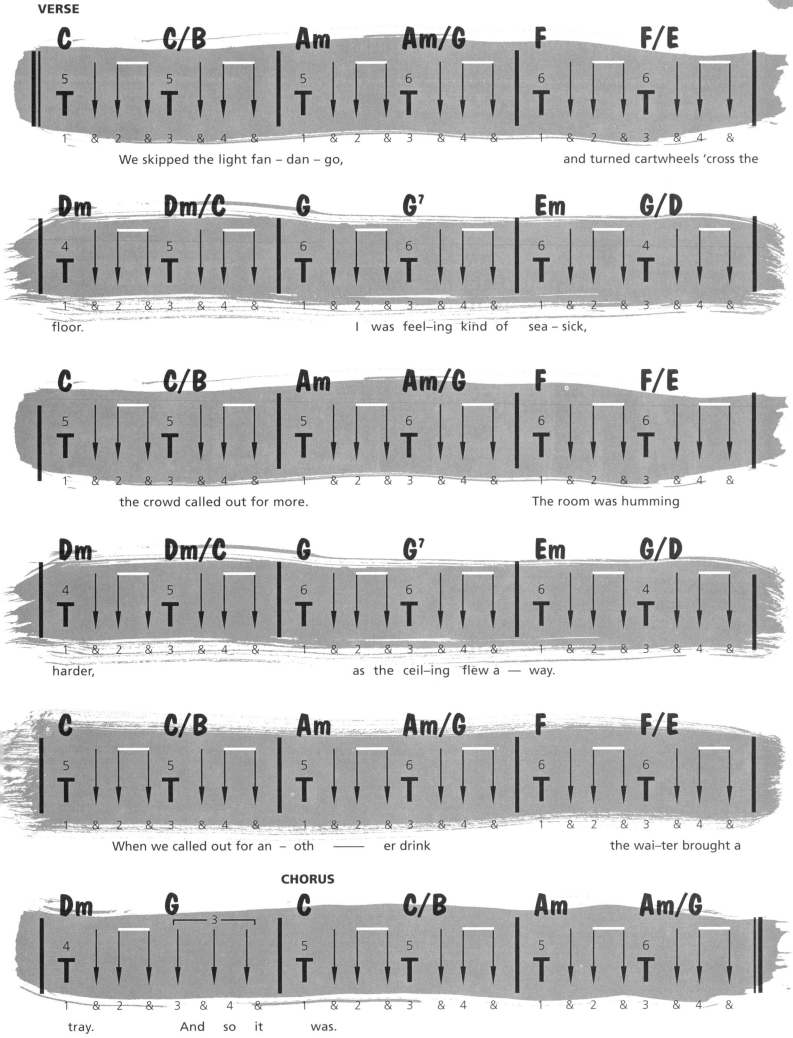

LAYLA
Words & Music by Eric Clapton & Jim Gordon

Eric Clapton

Layla" comes from Eric Clapton's 1970 album *Layla and Other Assorted Love Songs,* under the name of Derek and the Dominoes.

A chart hit several times, it remains one of rock's most dynamic love songs. You already know all the chord shapes for this song. The **G♯m7** and **C♯m7** chords use the same shapes as **F♯m7** and **Bm7**, both moved up two frets. The **B♭** can be played by taking a **B** chord and moving it down one fret. The main challenge here is the strumming.

In the verse, "**Layla**" makes partial use of a 16th strum, so keep your strumming hand relaxed. The chorus rhythm is less of a rock pattern, and more of a soul influence.

When you've gotten used to the chords you can try the famous intro riff. The hammer-ons and pull-offs in the first bar are optional, but help you to play faster.

GUITAR RIFF

VERSE

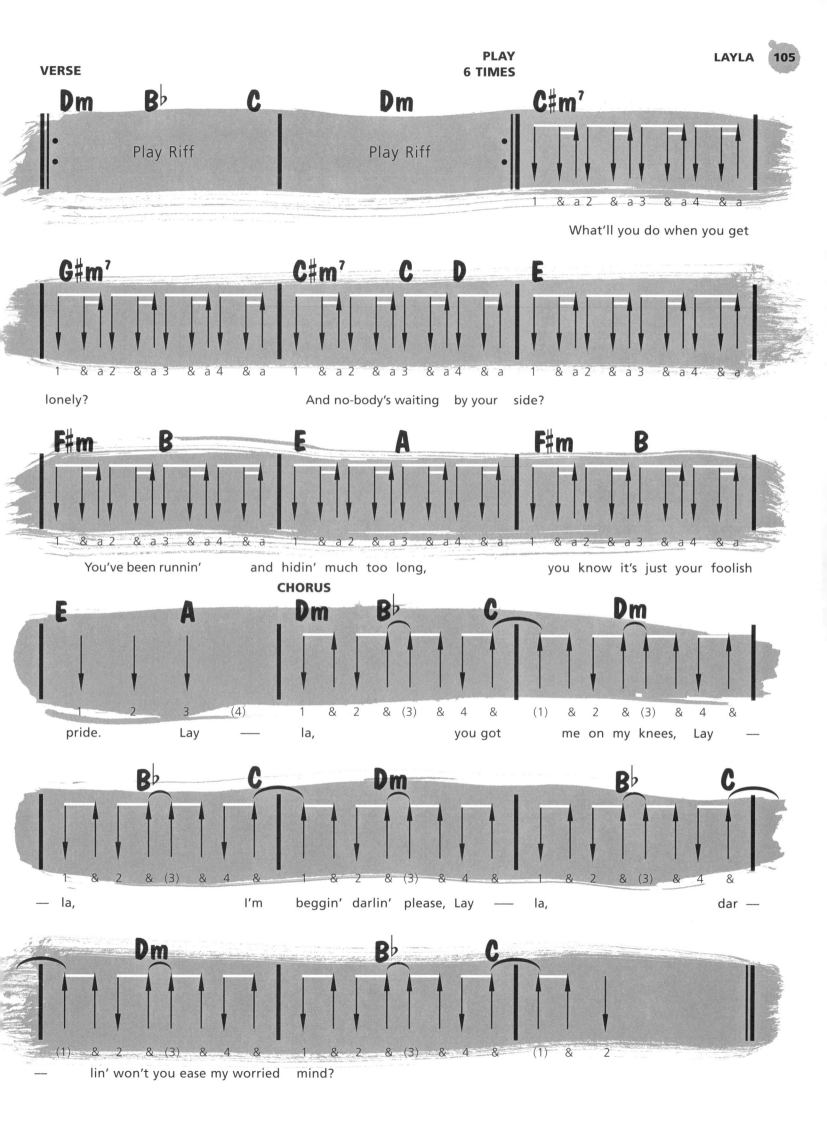

Dm   B♭   C   Dm   C#m⁷

Play Riff   Play Riff

1 & a2 & a3 & a4 & a

What'll you do when you get

G#m⁷   C#m⁷ C D   E

1 & a2 & a3 & a4 & a   1 & a2 & a3 & a4 & a   1 & a2 & a3 & a4 & a

lonely?   And no-body's waiting   by your   side?

F#m   B   E   A   F#m   B

1 & a2 & a3 & a4 & a   1 & a2 & a3 & a4 & a   1 & a2 & a3 & a4 & a

You've been runnin'   and hidin' much too long,   you know it's just your foolish

CHORUS

E   A   Dm   B♭   C   Dm

1   2   3   (4)   1 & 2 & (3) & 4 &   (1) & 2 & (3) & 4 &

pride.   Lay —— la,   you got   me on my knees, Lay —

B♭   C   Dm   B♭   C

1 & 2 & (3) & 4 &   1 & 2 & (3) & 4 &   1 & 2 & (3) & 4 &

— la,   I'm beggin' darlin' please, Lay — la,   dar —

Dm   B♭   C

(1) & 2 & (3) & 4 &   1 & 2 & (3) & 4 &   (1) & 2

— lin' won't you ease my worried   mind?

Bryan Adams

(EVERYTHING I DO) I DO IT FOR YOU

from the Motion Picture
Robin Hood: Prince Of Thieves

Words & Music by Bryan Adams, Robert John Lange & Michael Kamen

From the Kevin Costner film *Robin Hood*, "Everything I Do" proved to be one of the biggest hits of the 1990s.

There are no new chords here, so you can concentrate on the alternating picking and strumming patterns. For the verse chords, you can get away with holding down partial shapes as you should only strum the top three strings (in between picking the D string).

2 BAR CLICK + 4 BAR PIANO INTRO
VERSE (First time around, strum 1st beat of each bar only for bars 1-8)

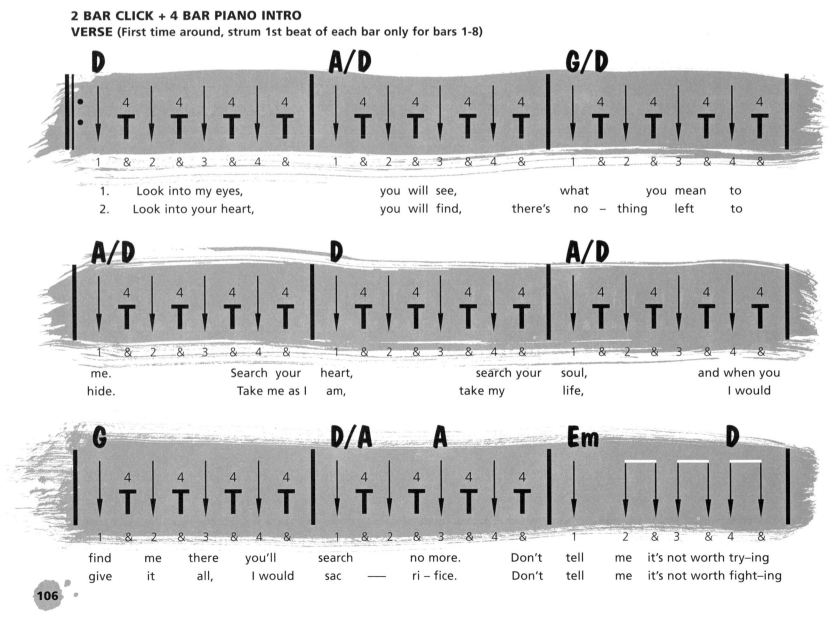

106

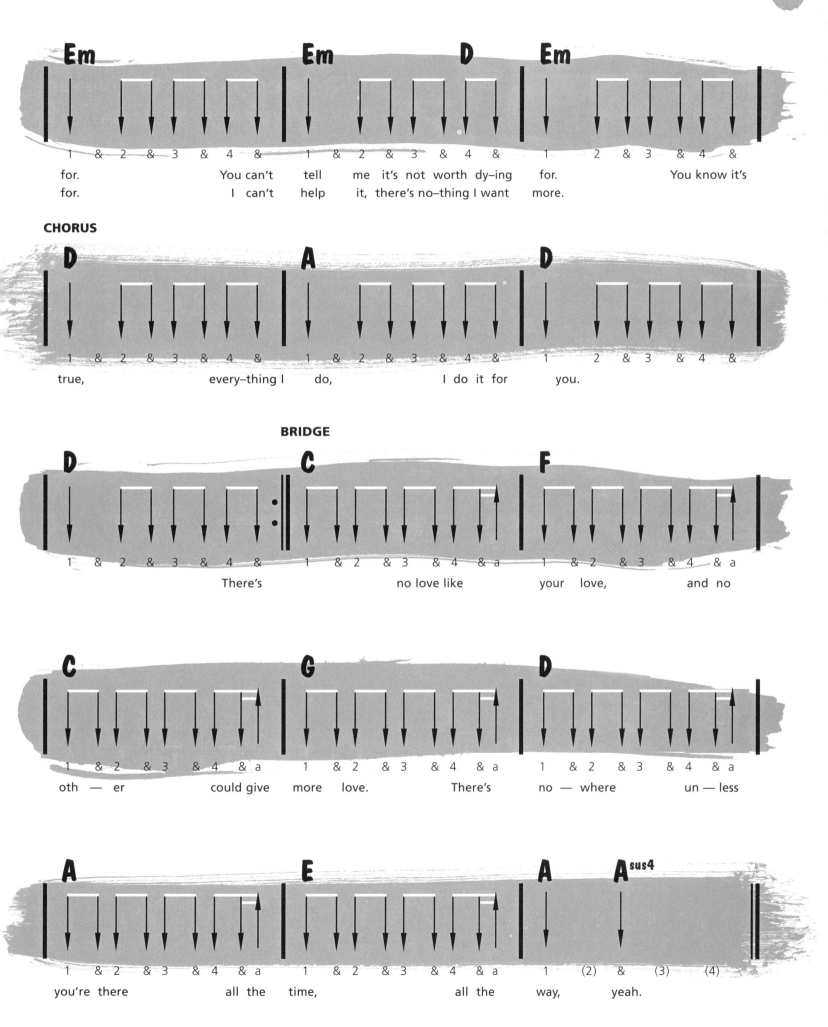

Em | **Em** | **D** | **Em**

1 & 2 & 3 & 4 & | 1 & 2 & 3 & 4 & | 1 2 & 3 & 4 &

for. You can't tell me it's not worth dy–ing for. You know it's
for. I can't help it, there's no–thing I want more.

CHORUS

D | **A** | **D**

1 & 2 & 3 & 4 & | 1 & 2 & 3 & 4 & | 1 2 & 3 & 4 &

true, every–thing I do, I do it for you.

BRIDGE

D | **C** | **F**

1 & 2 & 3 & 4 & | 1 & 2 & 3 & 4 & a | 1 & 2 & 3 & 4 & a

There's no love like your love, and no

C | **G** | **D**

1 & 2 & 3 & 4 & a | 1 & 2 & 3 & 4 & a | 1 & 2 & 3 & 4 & a

oth — er could give more love. There's no — where un — less

A | **E** | **A** **A**sus4

1 & 2 & 3 & 4 & a | 1 & 2 & 3 & 4 & a | 1 (2) & (3) (4)

you're there all the time, all the way, yeah.

MESSAGE IN A BOTTLE
Music & Lyrics by Sting

Well, it's now time for a challenge. There are no new chords in "Message In A Bottle," but the guitar riff itself will be an excellent stretching exercise.

Think of it as four three-note figures. Drop your thumb lower behind the neck to open up your hand. Play the first note with your 1st finger, the second with your 2nd finger and the third with your 4th finger. This riff is played throughout the verse.

If you are strumming this song watch out for the damping in the chorus. You need to mute the strings a little and emphasize the lower notes of each chord until you get to **C♯m7**. At the end of the chorus, get ready for the riff again.

The Police

RIFF

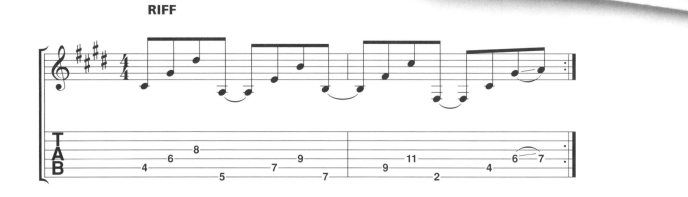

VERSE & RIFF

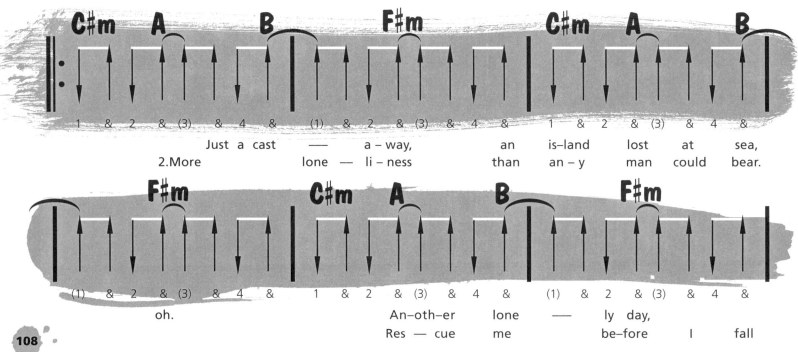

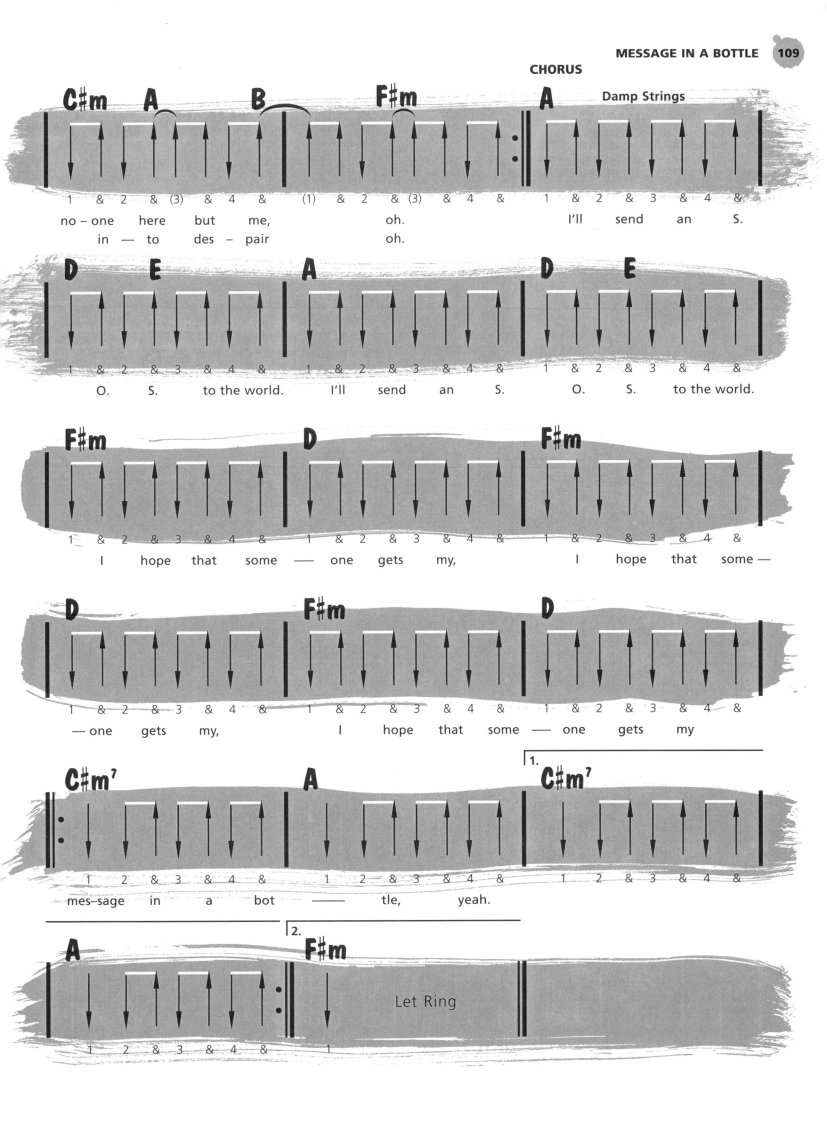

Dire Straits

SULTANS OF SWING
Words & Music by Mark Knopfler

This early hit for Dire Straits is justly renowned for its intricate lead guitar fills and solos.

To play the rhythm part you need to use that percussive "click" technique used before. Here I will mention another way of doing it. Wherever you see a little cross (**x**) on a beat let the side of your strumming hand hit the strings a fraction of a second before the pick does. If you make your hand strike the strings inward toward the guitar an extra percussive noise is made by the strings themselves hitting the metal frets. So the first verse bar is strummed: 1 "click" & 3 & "click" &.

Here in TAB is the famous chorus **riff**. Notice the chords only have three notes. Mark Knopfler plays with his fingers rather than a pick, so it is natural to play triads by striking them with the thumb and first and second fingers.

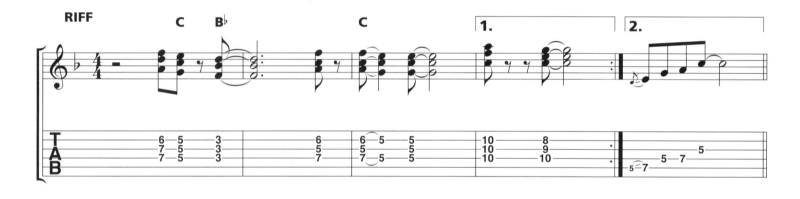

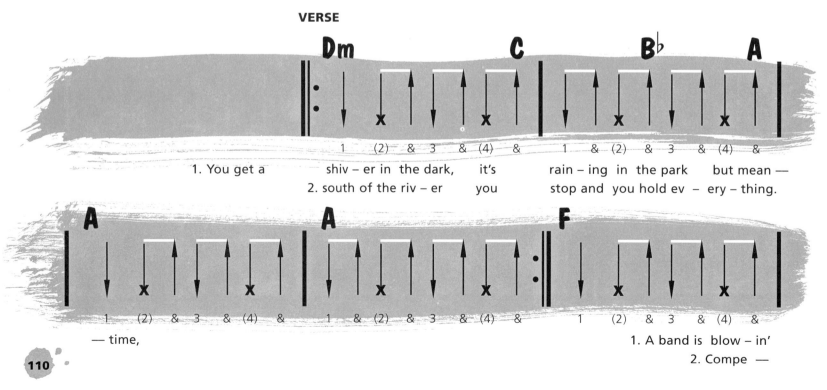

1. You get a shiv – er in the dark, it's rain – ing in the park but mean —
2. south of the riv – er you stop and you hold ev – ery – thing.

— time,

1. A band is blow – in'
2. Compe —

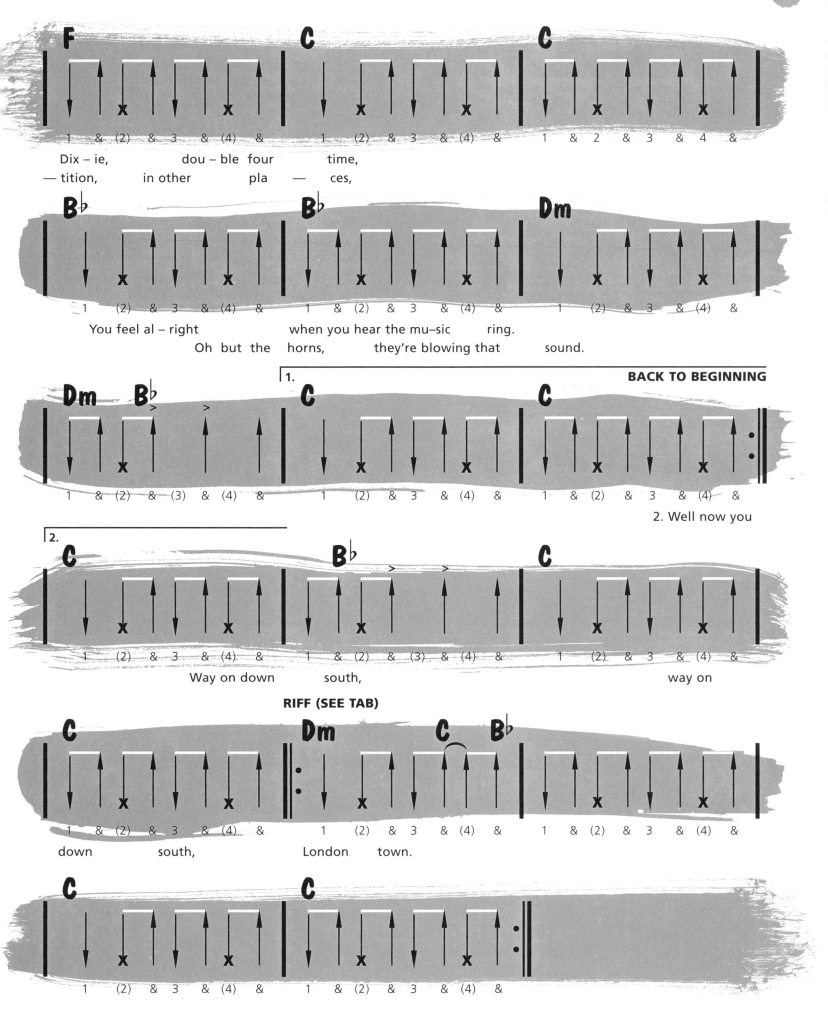

MULDER AND SCULLY
Words & Music by Mark Roberts, Owen Powell, Paul Jones, Cerys Matthews & Aled Richards

To play the opening track of Catatonia's *International Velvet* album you will need several new chord shapes: Amaj7, A6, Dmaj7, C#7 and an alternative shape for A major, A*.

Most of the strumming for this song is easy. The only tricky bit is the first bar with its quick change of chords and the 16th notes. Listen carefully to the CD to help you get a feel for the timing.

A* Chord

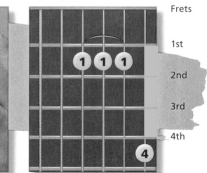

Amaj7 Chord

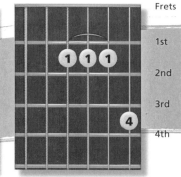

A6 Chord

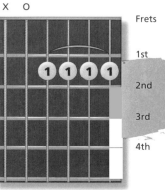

Dmaj7 Chord

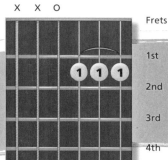

C#7 Chord

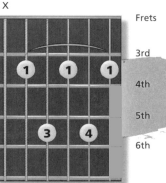

2 BAR CLICK INTRO   **VERSE**

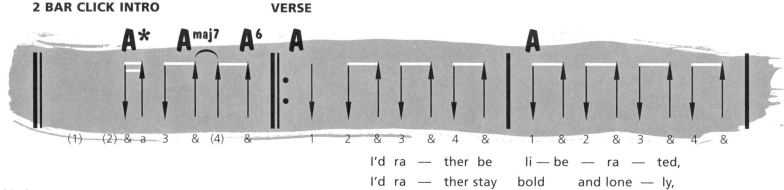

I'd ra — ther be   li — be — ra — ted,
I'd ra — ther stay   bold   and lone — ly,

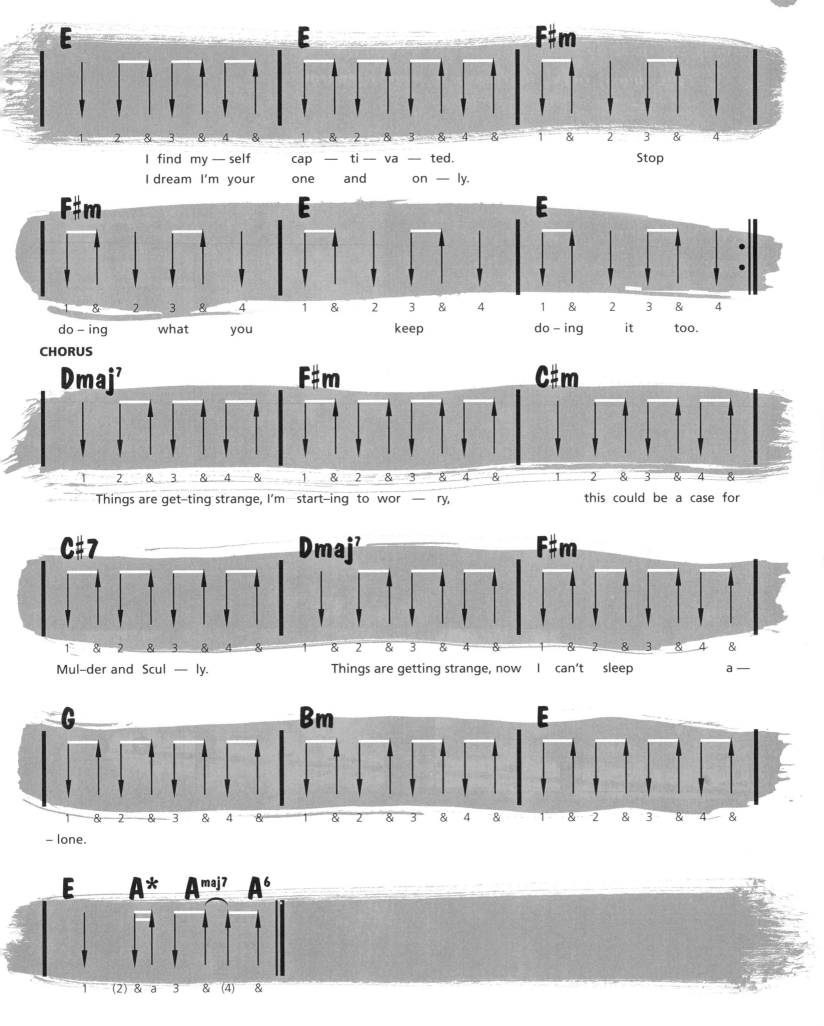

GOODBYE YELLOW BRICK ROAD
Words & Music by Elton John & Bernie Taupin

G#7 Chord

The title track of Elton John's 1973 double album is a slow tempo song with plenty of chord changes. However, all but one of the chords you already know. The new chord is G#7, shown here.

This shape is derived from the full barre major chord **F**, with the little finger lifted off to create the 7th.

Frets
3rd
4th
5th
6th

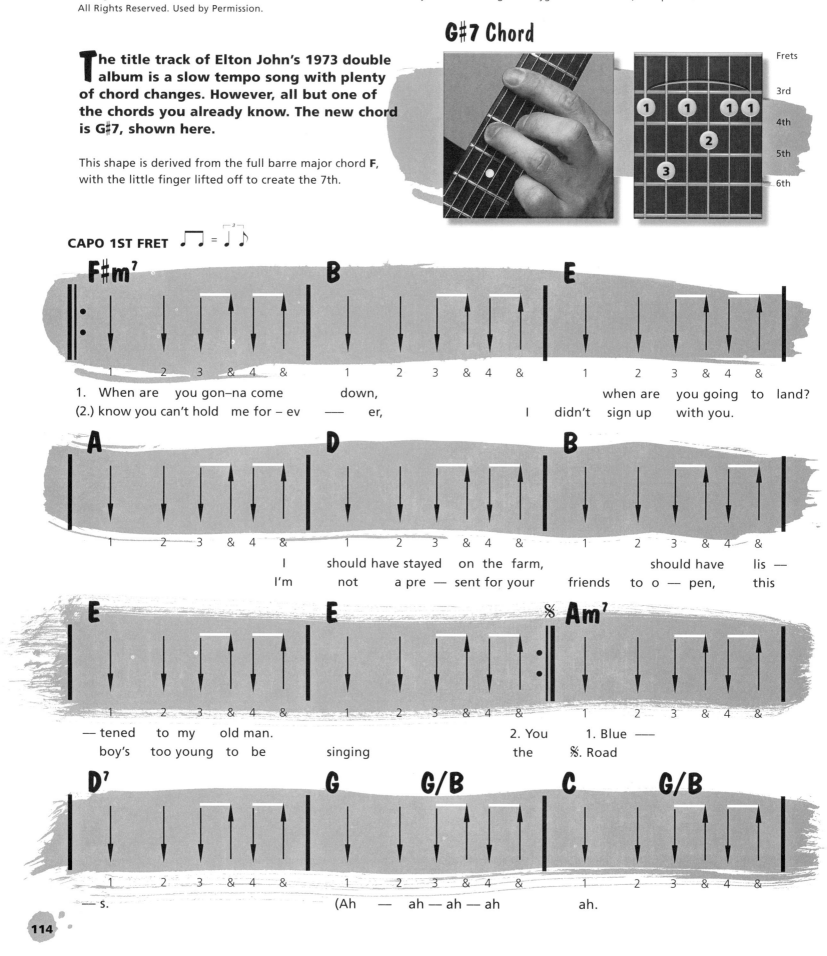

CAPO 1ST FRET

1. When are you gon–na come down, when are you going to land?
(2.) know you can't hold me for – ev — er, I didn't sign up with you.

I should have stayed on the farm, should have lis —
I'm not a pre — sent for your friends to o — pen, this

— tened to my old man. 1. Blue —
boy's too young to be singing 2. You the %. Road

— s.
(Ah — ah — ah — ah ah.

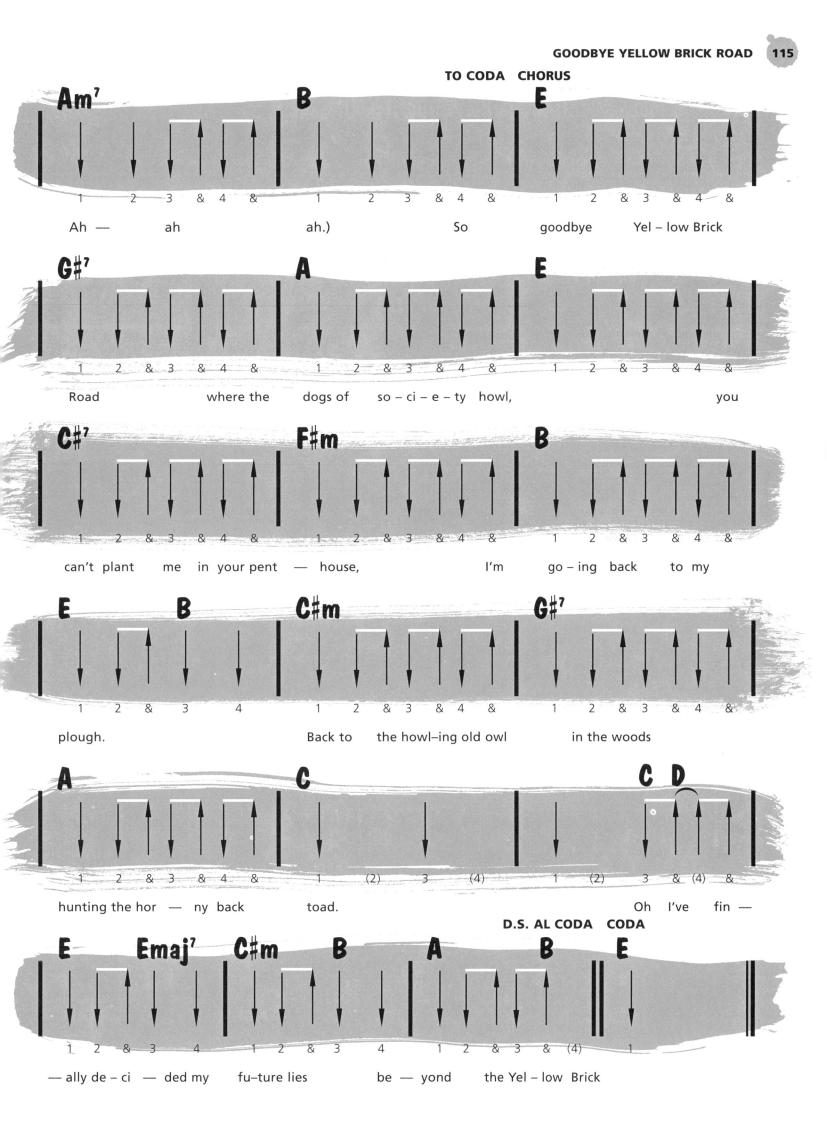

KNOWING ME, KNOWING YOU
Words & Music by Benny Andersson, Björn Ulvaeus & Stig Anderson

You will notice a Bsus2 in the music for this Abba song. It occurs just before the chorus on the word "goodbye."

This chord is based on the **Asus2** open shape, where you simply hold down **A** and take your finger off the **B** string. Here it is turned into a moveable barre chord. The **sus2** chord is not as tense as the **sus4**.

Note that the second to last bar is in 2/4 time, which means that you count 1&2& only, before returning to 4/4 as you play the **D** chord in the last bar on the word "do." You will recognize the solo riff in the tablature from the link between the chorus and the verse on the original recording.

Bsus2 Chord

CAPO 3RD FRET
SOLO RIFF

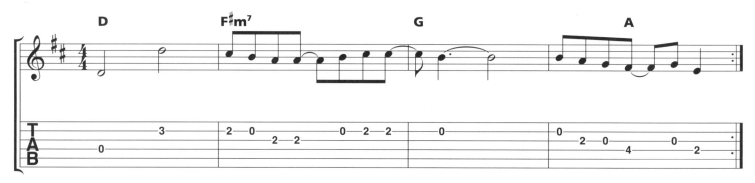

CAPO 3RD FRET

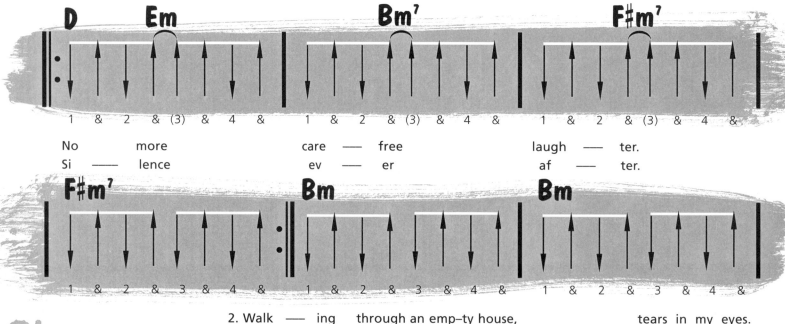

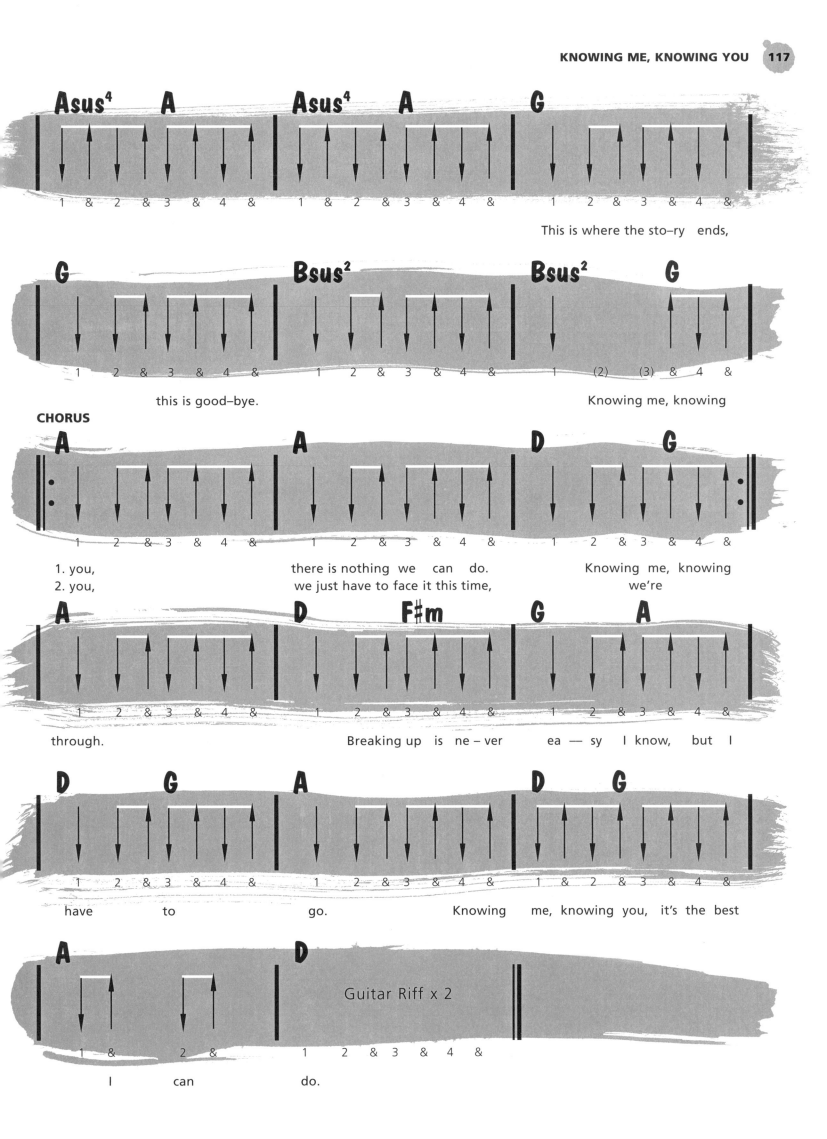

ANGELS

Words & Music by Robert Peter Williams & Guy Chambers

Robbie Williams achieved huge chart success with this anthemic ballad, and we've provided the entire song this time.

This song has a slightly more complicated structure as a result. On the second time through you can either stick to our suggested strumming pattern, or continue the "chorus" strumming pattern. Also, jump straight from bar 4 to bar 9, leaving out the bars in between.

The instruction "Da Capo" at the end of the chorus means "back to the beginning." After the solo and chorus repeat, you finish there at the "Fine" instruction.

The two new inversions below will complement the **G/B**, **C/E** and **D/F♯** you already know. Remember that if you find inversions awkward you can always replace them with the ordinary root position version of the chord.

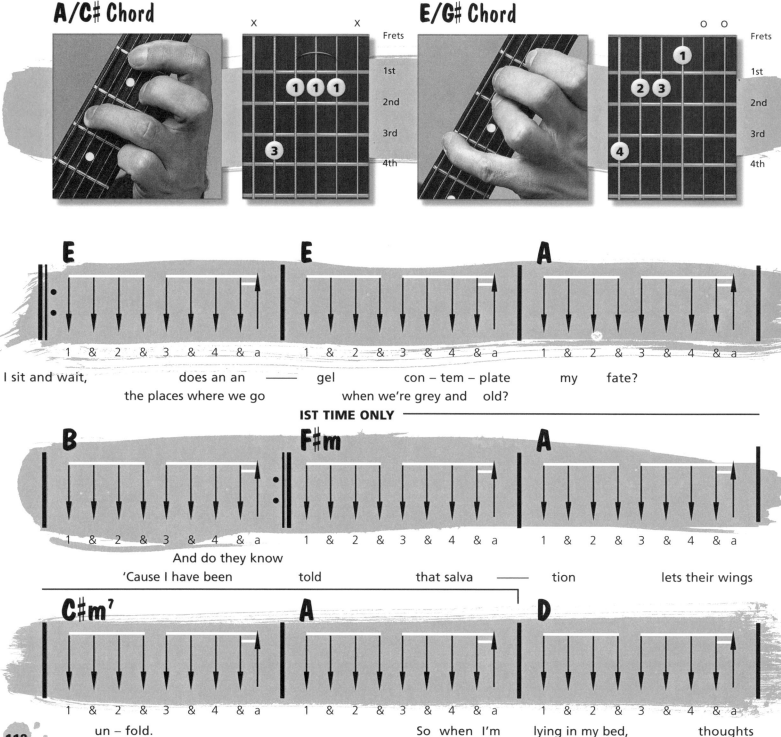

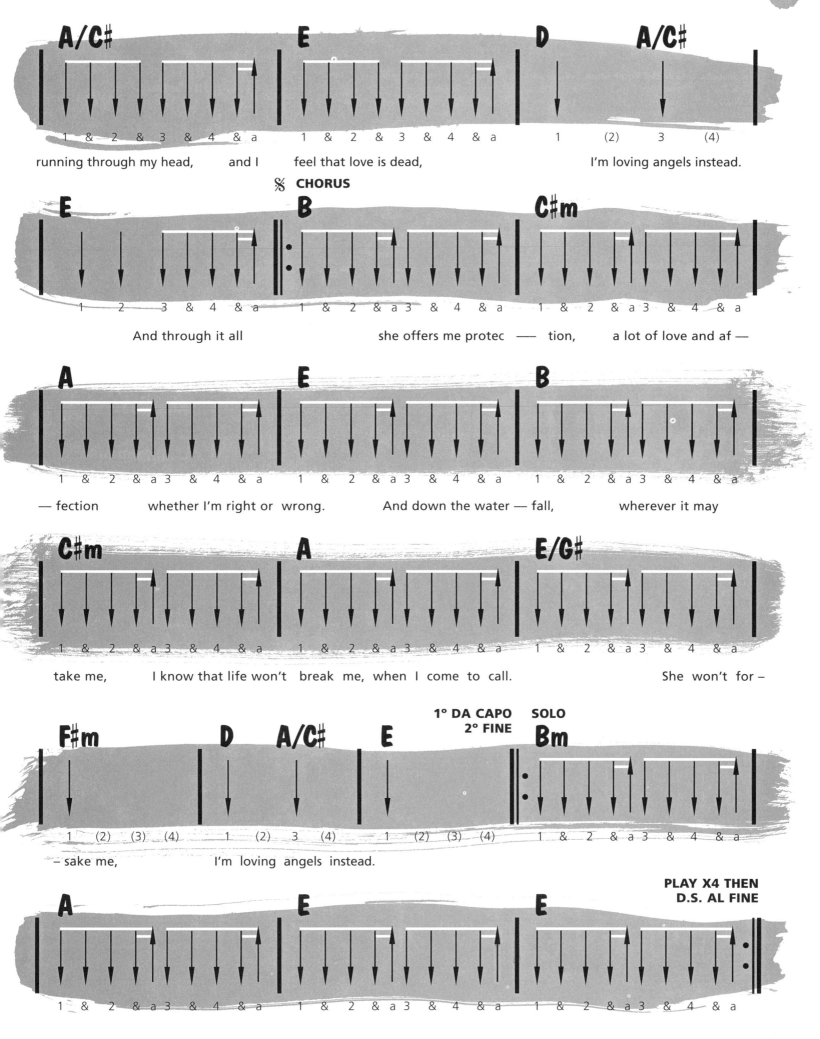

running through my head, and I feel that love is dead, I'm loving angels instead.

CHORUS

And through it all she offers me protec — tion, a lot of love and af —

— fection whether I'm right or wrong. And down the water — fall, wherever it may

take me, I know that life won't break me, when I come to call. She won't for —

1° DA CAPO
2° FINE **SOLO**

— sake me, I'm loving angels instead.

PLAY X4 THEN
D.S. AL FINE

LUCKY MAN
By Greg Lake

Progressive-rock supergroup Emerson, Lake & Palmer had a hit with "Lucky Man" in 1971. It is featured on their self-titled album of that same year.

This song begins with a famous arpeggio that uses some interesting chord variations. The arpeggio is written out for you in the TAB below. You can see that the first two notes are doubled by playing a G on the 5th fret of the 4th string and then another G on the open 3rd string. This keeps the picking pattern the same for both chords.

You can play this arpeggio throughout the verses, or strum the chords. Notice that this tune has only three beats in each measure, with a gentle 1 2 & 3 pattern, like a waltz. The last line of the chorus decorates the D major chord with a **sus4** and a **sus2.** These three chords frequently appear together because they are easy to play and sound great.

Emerson, Lake & Palmer

INTRO ARPEGGIO

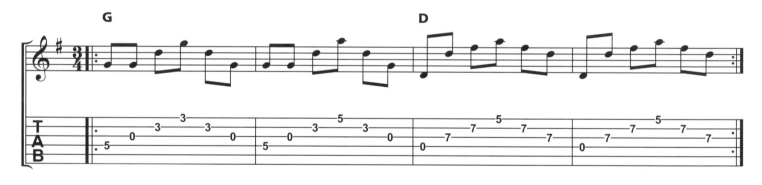

VERSE

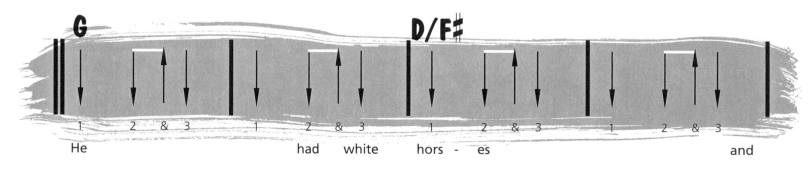

He ... had white hors - es ... and

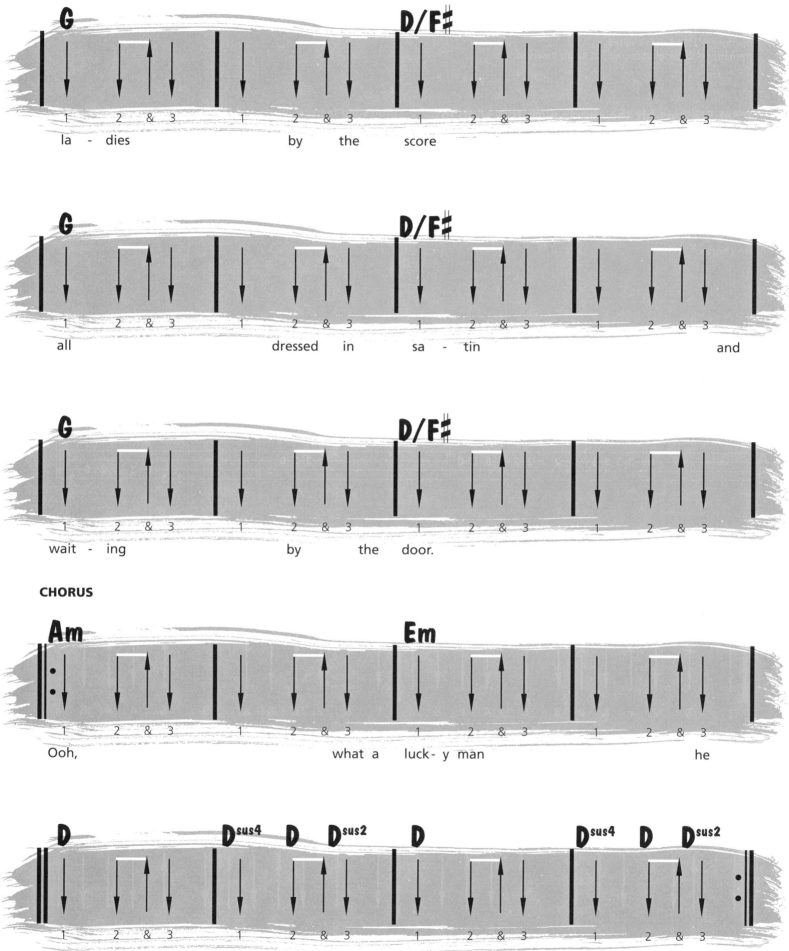

WILD WORLD
Words & Music by Cat Stevens

Cat Stevens hit the charts with this song in 1971 when it reached No. 11. It is featured on his multi-platinum album *Tea For The Tillerman*.

Take this song slowly for the 1 & 2-e-&-a 3 & 4-e-&-a pattern, and feel free to vary the accents on your strums. Watch out for the last measure before the chorus—it contains only two beats. Just keep the count in your head and it will flow seamlessly into the chorus.

This song features three guitar fills at the chorus. All three are written out in TAB below. **Fill 1** is a descending line across the 2-beat measure into the chorus. **Fill 2** is a faster run right down the scale that leads from the **F chord** to the **G chord**. The last fill, **Fill 3,** is a turnaround lick that links up both lines of the chorus. Use down-up-down-up alternate picking for all of these lines.

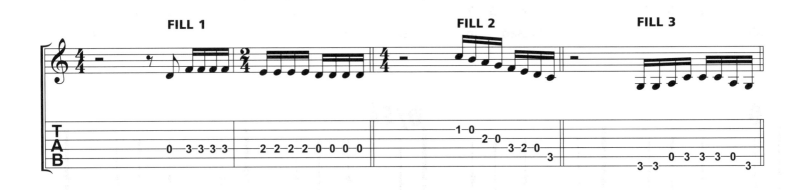

FILL 1   FILL 2   FILL 3

VERSE

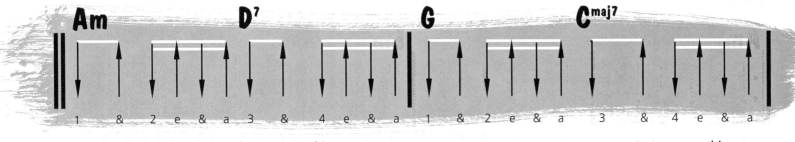

Now that I've   lost ev-'ry-thing   to you,   you   say you wan-na start some - thing new

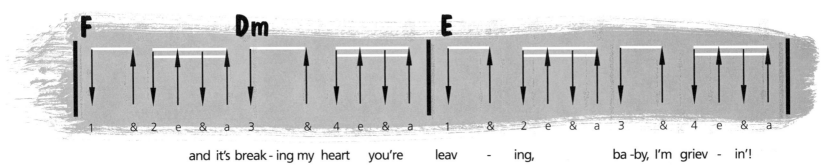

and it's break-ing my heart   you're   leav   -   ing,   ba -by, I'm griev - in'!

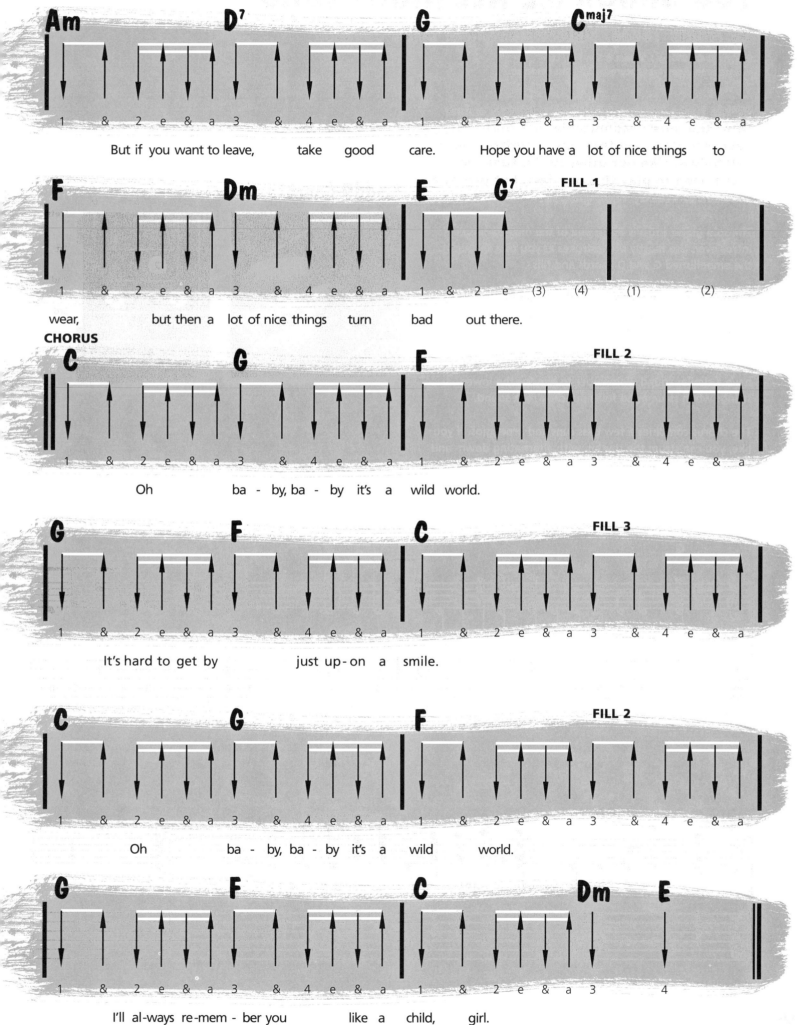

But if you want to leave,   take   good   care.   Hope you have a lot of nice things   to

wear,   but then a lot of nice things   turn   bad   out there.

CHORUS

Oh   ba - by, ba - by it's a   wild world.

It's hard to get by   just up - on a smile.

Oh   ba - by, ba - by it's a   wild   world.

I'll al-ways re-mem - ber you   like a   child,   girl.

YOU SHOOK ME ALL NIGHT LONG

By Angus Young, Malcolm Young & Brian Johnson

This huge hit for AC/DC also boasts a few of the most recognizable rock guitar riffs ever recorded, and they are all written out in TAB below. Like our other AC/DC tune, you don't need to play this one fast, but just at a moderate steady rock groove.

The solo guitar intro is easily one of the most famous intros ever. Use mostly downstrokes as you pick through the embellished G and D chords and fills.

The verse uses a new chord: **Cadd9**. The **add9** chord is basically a major chord with the ninth note of the scale added on top. The ninth is technically also the second, but in this case we are adding a note to the chord instead of replacing a note, like in the **sus2** chord. The two chords do have a similar sound. Remember to aim for the lower strings when strumming for a punchier rock sound.

The chorus combines a few bass runs and arpeggios. If you like, you can strum the rhythm with alternating down- and upstrokes as indicated.

Cadd9 Chord

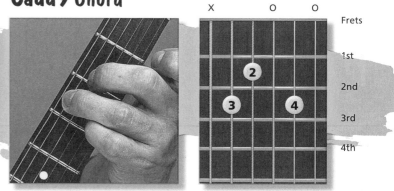

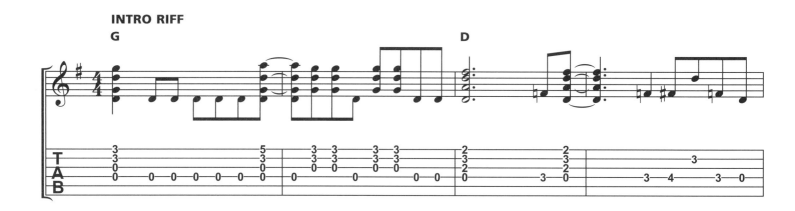

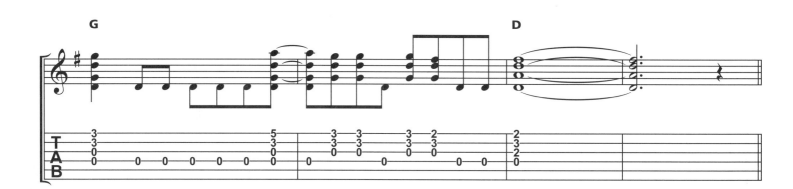

VERSE RIFF

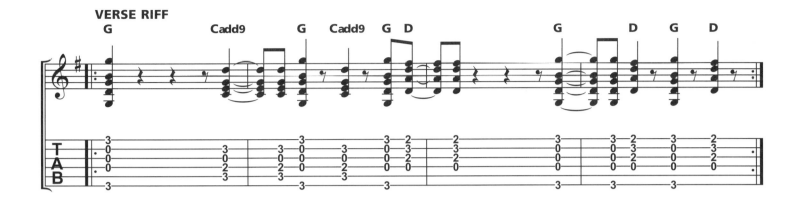

CHORUS RIFF

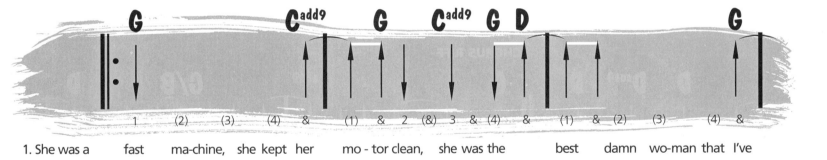

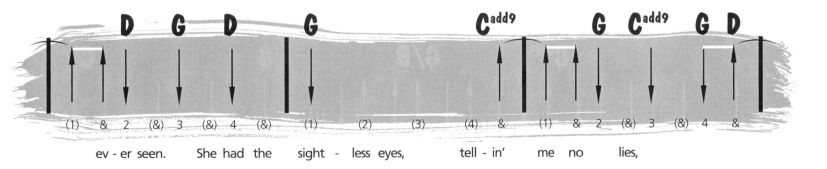

1. She was a fast ma-chine, she kept her mo-tor clean, she was the best damn wo-man that I've

ev - er seen. She had the sight - less eyes, tell - in' me no lies,

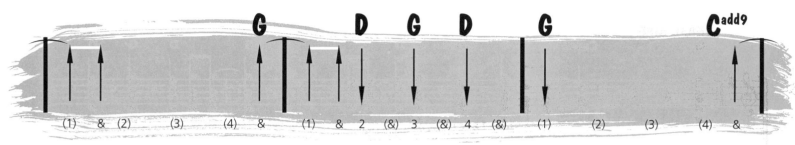

Knock - in' me out   with those A - mer - i - can   thighs.   Tak - in'   more than her share   had me

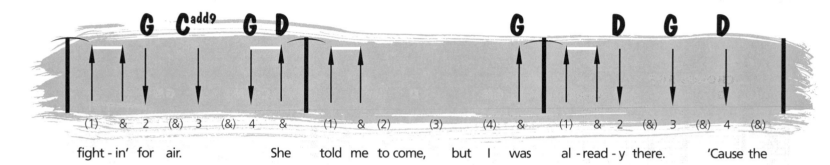

fight - in' for air.   She   told me to come,   but I was   al - read - y there.   'Cause the

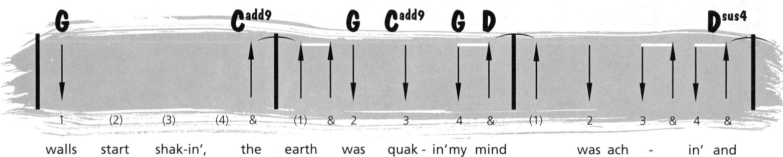

walls   start   shak - in',   the   earth   was   quak - in'my mind   was ach - in' and

CHORUS RIFF

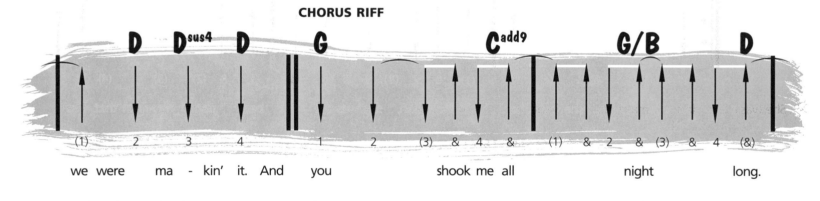

we were   ma - kin' it. And   you   shook me all   night   long.

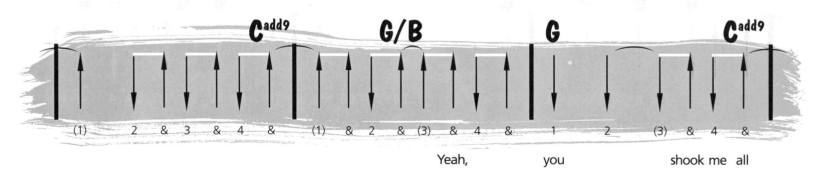

Yeah,   you   shook me all

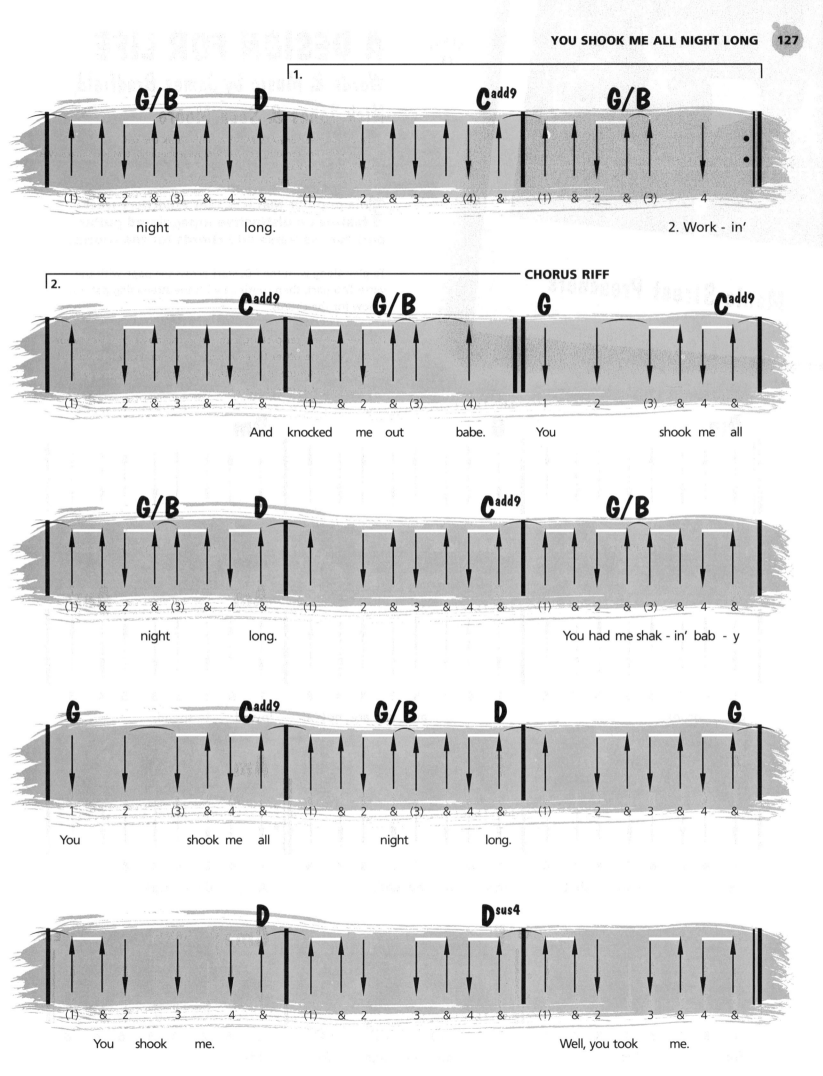

Manic Street Preachers

TRACK 19

A DESIGN FOR LIFE
Words & Music by James Bradfield, Nick Jones & Sean Moore

This popular Manic Street Preachers track features a distinctive arpeggiated guitar part for the verse and chords for the chorus.

To play along with the CD, start across the page with the verse TAB part, then continue with the strumming pattern below for the chorus.

For the TAB finger-picking part, play the bass note with your thumb and the other three notes with your 1st, 2nd and 3rd fingers in sequence. It is possible to play it just with a pick, but pick and fingers is easier.

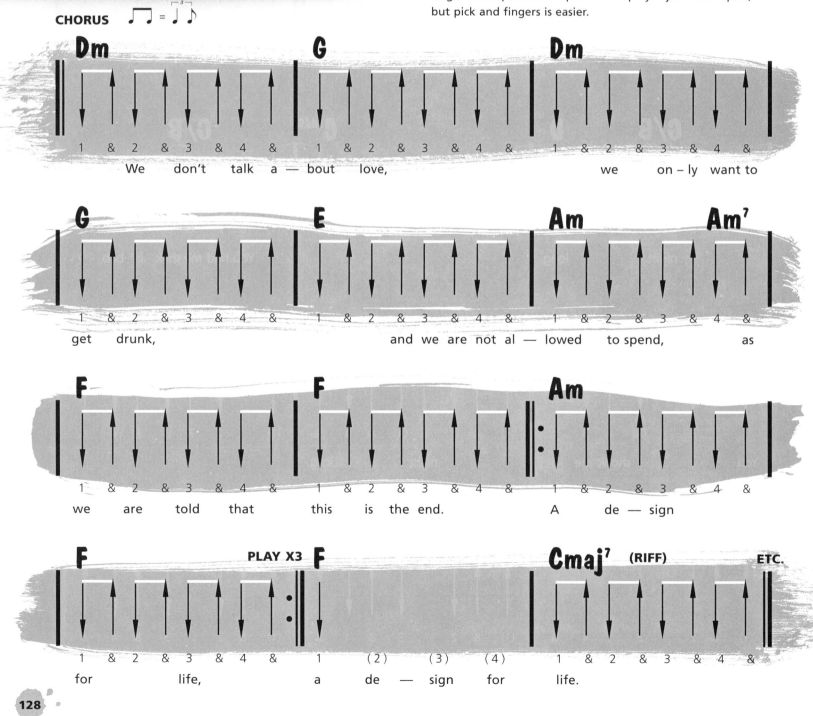

2 BAR CLICK INTRO
VERSE: GUITAR PART

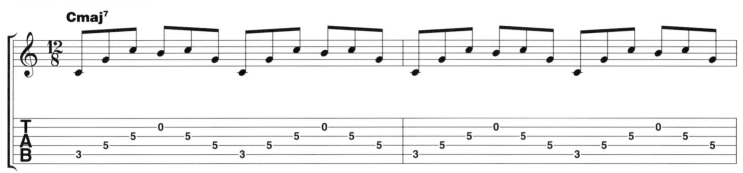

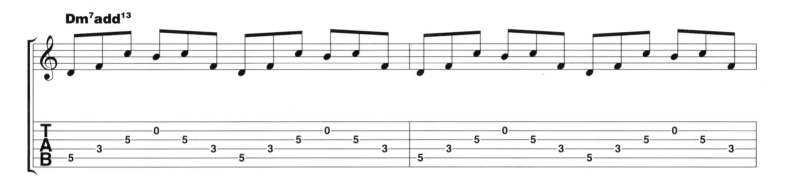

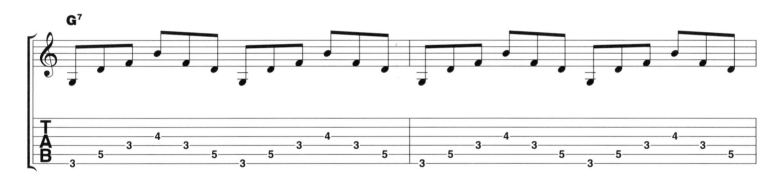

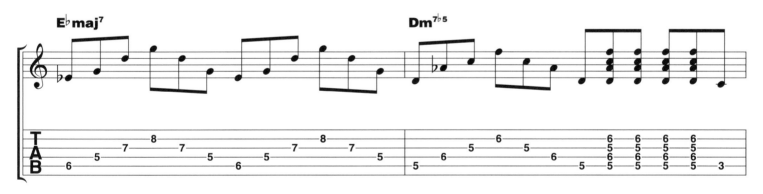

GO TO CHORUS
AFTER REPEAT

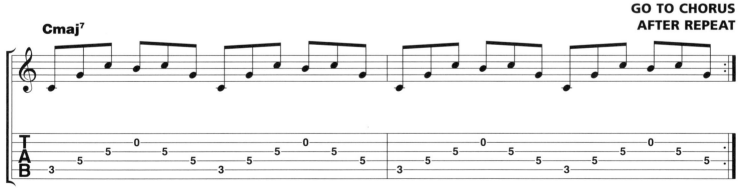

ADDITIONAL LYRICS

MRS. ROBINSON

Intro
Di di di di di di di di di di di di di
Doo doo doo doo doo doo doo
doo doo
Di di di di di di di di di di di di di

Chorus
And here's to you, Mrs. Robinson
Jesus loves you more than you will
know (wo, wo, wo)
God bless you please, Mrs. Robinson
Heaven holds a place for those
who pray
(Hey, hey, hey... hey, hey, hey).

Verse 1
We'd like to know a little bit about
you for our files
We'd like to help you learn to help
yourself
Look around you, all you see are
sympathetic eyes
Stroll around the grounds until you
feel at home.

Chorus

Verse 2
Hide it in a hiding place where no one
ever goes
Put it in your pantry with your
cupcakes
It's a little secret, just the Robinsons'
affair
Most of all, you've got to hide it from
the kids.

Chorus

Verse 3
Sitting on a sofa on a Sunday
afternoon
Going to the candidates' debate
Laugh about it, shout about it
When you've got to choose.
Ev'ry way you look at it, you lose.

Chorus 2
Where have you gone, Joe DiMaggio?
A nation turns its lonely eyes to you
(woo, woo, woo)
What's that you say, Mrs. Robinson?
Joltin' Joe has left and gone away
(Hey, hey, hey... hey, hey, hey).

YELLOW

Verse 1
Look at the stars
Look how they shine for you
And everything you do
Yeah, they were all yellow.

I came alive
I wrote a song for you
And all the things you do
And it was yellow.
So then I took my turn
Oh, what a thing to've done
And it was all yellow.

Chorus
Your skin, oh yeah your skin
and bones
Turn into something beautiful
And you know, you know I love you so
You know I love you so.

Verse 2
I swam across
I jumped across for you
Oh, what a thing to do
'Cause you were all yellow.

I drew a line, I drew a line for you
Oh, what a thing to do
And it was all yellow.

Chorus 2
And your skin, oh yeah your skin and
bones
Turn into something beautiful
And you know for you I'd bleed
myself dry
For you I'd bleed myself dry.

Coda
It's true, look how they shine for you
Look how they shine for you
Look how they shine for
Look how they shine for you
Look how they shine for you
Look how they shine.

Look at the stars
Look how they shine for you
And all the things that you do.

A WHITER SHADE OF PALE

Verse 1
We skipped the light fandango
Turned cartwheels 'cross the floor
I was feeling kind of seasick
The crowd called out for more
The room was humming harder
As the ceiling flew away
When we called out for another drink
The waiter brought a tray.

Chorus
And so it was that later
As the miller told his tale
That her face at first just ghostly
Turned a whiter shade of pale.

Verse 2
She said, "There is no reason
And the truth is plain to see"
But I wandered through my playing
cards
And would not let her be
One of sixteen vestal virgins
Who were leaving for the coast
And although my eyes were opened
They might just as well be closed

Chorus

LAYLA

Verse 1
What'll you do when you get lonely?
And no-body's waiting by your side
You been runnin' and hidin' much
too long
You know it's just your foolish pride.

Chorus
Layla, you got me on my knees
Layla, I'm beggin' darlin' please
Layla, darlin' won't you ease my
worried mind?

Verse 2
I tried to give you consolation
When your old man had let you down
Like a fool, I fell in love with you
You turned my whole world upside
down.

Chorus

Verse 3
Let's make the best of the situation
Before I finally go insane
Please don't say we'll never find a way
Don't tell me all my love's in vain.

Chorus to fade

(EVERYTHING I DO) I DO IT FOR YOU

Verse 1
Look into my eyes, you will see
What you mean to me
Search your heart, search your soul
And when you find me there you'll
search no more
Don't tell me it's not worth trying for
You can't tell me it's not worth
dying for
You know it's true
Everything I do, I do it for you.

Verse 2
Look into your heart, and you will find
There's nothing there to hide
Take me as I am, take my life
I would give it all, I would sacrifice

Don't tell me it's not worth fighting
for
I can't help it, there's nothing I want
more
You know it's true
Everything I do, I do it for you.

Bridge
There's no love like your love
And no other could give more love
There's nowhere unless you're there
All the time, all the way.

Solo

Verse 3
Oh, you can't tell me it's not worth
trying for
I can't help it, there's nothing I want
more
Yeah, I would fight for you, I'd lie for
you
Walk the wire for you, yeah I'd die for
you
You know it's true
Everything I do
Oh I do it for you.

Coda (ad lib to fade)

MESSAGE IN A BOTTLE

Verse 1
Just a castaway, an island lost at sea-o
Another lonely day, no one here but
me-o
More loneliness than any man could
bear
Rescue me before I fall into despair-o.

Chorus
I'll send an S.O.S. to the world
I'll send an S.O.S. to the world
I hope that someone gets my
I hope that someone gets my
I hope that someone gets my
Message in a bottle, yeah.
Message in a bottle, yeah.

Verse 2
A year has passed since I wrote my
note
But I should have known this right
from the start
Only hope can keep me together
Love can mend your life but love can
break your heart.

Chorus

Message in a bottle, yeah.
Message in a bottle.

Verse 3
Walked out this morning I don't
believe what I saw
A hundred billion bottles washed up
on the shore
Seems I'm not alone in being alone
Hundred billion castaways looking for
a home.

Chorus

Message in a bottle, yeah.
Message in a bottle.

Coda (repeat to fade)
I'm sending out an S.O.S.

SULTANS OF SWING

Verse 1
You get a shiver in the dark, it's
raining in the park
But meantime, south of the river
You stop and you hold everything
A band is blowin' Dixie, double four
time
You feel all right when you hear the
music ring.

Verse 2
Well now you step inside
But you don't see too many faces
Comin' in out of the rain to hear the
jazz go down
Competition, in other places
But the horns, they're blowin' that
sound
Way on down south, way on down
south, London Town.

Verse 3

You check out Guitar George, he knows all the chords
Mind he's strictly rhythm, he doesn't want to make it cry or sing
This and an old guitar is all he can afford
When he gets up under the lights to play his thing.

Verse 4

And Harry doesn't mind if he doesn't make the scene
He's got a daytime job, he's doin' all right
He can play the honky-tonk like anything
Savin' it up for Friday night
With the Sultans, with the Sultans of Swing.

Verse 5

And the crowd of young boys
They're foolin' around in the corner
Drunk and dressed in their best brown baggies and their platform soles
They don't give a damn about any trumpet-playin' band
It ain't what they call rock 'n' roll
And the Sultans, yeah the Sultans, they played Creole.

Instrumental

Verse 6

And then the man, he steps right up to the microphone
And says, at last, just as the time-bell rings:
"Good night now, it's time to go home."
And he makes it fast with one more thing:
"We are the Sultans, we are the Sultans of Swing."

MULDER AND SCULLY

Verse 1

I'd rather be liberated, I find myself captivated
Stop doing what you keep doing it too
I'd rather stay bold and lonely, I dream I'm your one and only
Stop doing what you keep doing it too.

Chorus

Things are getting strange, I'm starting to worry
This could be a case for Mulder and Scully
Things are getting strange, now I can't sleep alone.

Verse 2

I'd rather be jumping ship, I find myself jumping straight in
Stop doing what you keep doing it too
Forever be dozy and dim, I wake myself thinking of him
Stop doing what you keep doing it too.

Chorus

Bridge

My bed is made for two and there's nothing I can do
So tell me something I don't know
If my head is full of you is there nothing I can do?
Must we all march in two by two by two?

Verse 3

And as for some happy ending
I'd rather stay single and thin
Stop doing what you keep doing to me

Chorus x 2

Coda

So what have you got to say about that?
And what does someone do without love?
And what does someone do with love?
And what have you got to say about that?

GOODBYE YELLOW BRICK ROAD

Verse 1

When are you gonna come down
When are you gonna land?
I should have stayed on the farm
Should have listened to my old man.

You know you can't hold me forever
I didn't sign up with you
I'm not a present for your friends to open
This boy's too young to be singing the blues.

Chorus

So goodbye Yellow Brick Road
Where the dogs of society howl
You can't plant me in your penthouse
I'm going back to my plough
Back to the howling old owl in the woods
Hunting the horny back toad
Oh I've finally decided my future lies
Beyond the Yellow Brick Road.

Verse 2

What do you think you'll do then
I bet that'll shoot down your plane
It'll take you a couple of vodka and tonics
To set you on your feet again.

Maybe you'll get a replacement
There's plenty like me to be found
Mongrels who ain't got a penny
Sniffling for tidbits like you on the ground.

Chorus

KNOWING ME, KNOWING YOU

Verse 1

No more carefree laughter
Silence ever after
Walking through an empty house
Tears in my eyes
This is where the story ends
This is goodbye.

Chorus
Knowing me, knowing you
There is nothing we can do
Knowing me, knowing you
We just have to face it
This time we're through
Breaking up is never easy I know
But I have to go
Knowing me, knowing you
It's the best I can do.

Verse 2
Memories, good days, bad days
They'll be with me always
In these old familiar rooms children would play
Now there's only emptiness, nothing to say.

Chorus x 2

ANGELS

Verse 1
I sit and wait
Does an angel contemplate my fate
And do they know
The places where we go
When we're gray and old?
'Cause I have been told
That salvation lets their wings unfold
So when I'm lying in my bed
Thoughts running through my head
And I feel that love is dead
I'm loving angels instead.

Chorus
And through it all
She offers me protection
A lot of love and affection
Whether I'm right or wrong
And down the waterfall
Wherever it may take me
I know that life won't break me
When I come to call
She won't forsake me
I'm loving angels instead.

Verse 2
When I'm feeling weak
And my pain walks down a one-way street

I look above, and I know I'll always be blessed with love
And as the feeling grows
She brings flesh to my bones
And when love is dead
I'm loving angels instead.

Chorus

Solo

Chorus

LUCKY MAN

Verse 1
He had white horses
And ladies by the score
All dressed in satin
And waiting by the door

Chorus
Ooh, what a lucky man he was
Ooh, what a lucky man he was

Verse 2
White lace and feathers
They made up his bed
A gold-covered mattress
On which he was laid

Chorus

Instrumental

Verse 3
He went to fight wars
For his country and his king
Of his honor and his glory
The people would sing

Chorus

Verse 4
A bullet had found him
His blood ran as he cried
No money could save him
So he laid down and he died

Chorus

WILD WORLD

Verse 1
Now that I've lost everything to you
You say you wanna start something new
And it's breaking my heart you're leaving
Baby, I'm grievin'!
But if you want to leave, take good care
Hope you have a lot of nice things to wear
But then a lot of nice things turn bad out there

Chorus
Oh baby, baby it's a wild world
It's hard to get by just upon a smile
Oh baby, baby it's a wild world
I'll always remember you like a child, girl

Verse 2
You know I've seen a lot of what the world can do
And it's breaking my heart in two
Because I never want to see you sad, girl
Don't be a bad girl
But if you want to leave, take good care
Hope you make a lot of nice friends out there
But just remember there's a lot of bad and beware

Chorus

Verse 3
Baby, I love you
But if you want to leave, take good care
Hope you make a lot of nice friends out there
But just remember there's a lot of bad and beware

Chorus x 2

YOU SHOOK ME ALL NIGHT LONG

Verse 1
She was a fast machine, she kept her
motor clean
She was the best damn woman that
I've ever seen
She had the sightless eyes, tellin' me no
lies
Knockin' me out with those American
thighs
Takin' more than her share had me
fightin' for air
She told me to come but I was already
there
'Cause the walls start shakin', the earth
was quakin'
My mind was achin' and we were
makin' it

Chorus
And you shook me all night long
Yeah you shook me all night long

Verse 2
Workin' double time on the seduction
line
She was one of a kind, she's just mine
all mine
Wanted no applause, just another
course
Made a meal outta me and come back
for more
Had to cool me down to take another
round
Now I'm back in the ring to take
another swing
'Cause the walls was shakin', the earth
was quakin'
My mind was achin', and we were
makin' it

Chorus x 2

Instrumental

Chorus x 2

A DESIGN FOR LIFE

Verse 1
Libraries gave us power
Then work came and made us free
What price now
For a shallow piece of dignity?

Verse 2
I wish I had a bottle
Right here in my dirty face
To wear the scars
To show from where I came.

Chorus
We don't talk about love
We only want to get drunk
And we are not allowed to spend
As we are told that this is the end
A design for life, a design for life
A design for life, a design for life.

Verse 3
I wish I had a bottle
Right here in my pretty face
To wear the scars
To show from where I came.

Chorus x 2

The Complete Rock & Pop Guitar Player

CONCLUSION

Congratulations! Now that you have worked your way through the three parts of *The Complete Rock & Pop Guitar Player*, you are ready to explore the world of guitar playing in more depth.

• If you want to do more chord strumming check out the many titles in the popular *Chord Songbook* series.

• If you want to learn well-known songs and albums in more detail look for a band/artist matching folio which will show you solos and riffs note for note, or try the excellent *Play Guitar With...* series.

• If you want to improve your lead guitar playing, your ability to improvise, or delve into the wonderful world of altered tunings, have a look at the *FastForward* series. All *FastForward* books are equipped with a CD so you can hear the examples and play along.

CD Track List

1. Tuning Notes
2. Paperback Writer
3. Brimful Of Asha
4. Rock Around The Clock
5. I Wanna Be Adored
6. Stand By Me
7. Common People
8. That's Entertainment
9. Half The World Away
10. Driftwood
11. Sail Away
12. Wild Wood
13. Sunny Afternoon
14. While My Guitar Gently Weeps
15. Pinball Wizard
16. Mrs. Robinson
17. (Everything I Do) I Do It For You
18. Mulder And Scully
19. A Design For Life